The Message

A Time for Repair and
Reward in Texas Communities

Jack Daniel Foster, Jr.

Fulton Books
Meadville, PA

Published by Fulton Books 2024

ISBN 978-1-63860-658-1 (paperback)
ISBN 978-1-63860-659-8 (digital)

Printed in the United States of America

For my wife, Edwina Jena Foster. Who can find a virtuous wife? For her worth is far above rubies. The heart of her husband safely trusts her so he will have no lack of gain (Proverbs 31:10–11).

Dear Texans,

If you are reading *The Message: A Time for Repair and Reward in Texas Communities*, I hope there is a clear longing for something new and different because, if you are like me, I want a direction that will "push and pull" Texans in the same direction, instilling the belief that we can make a difference in both broken and unbroken lives. These writings capture the "soul essence" of how life can be lived throughout Texas, no matter the zip code, and begin to honor our commitment to one another in a way that will forevermore strengthen Texas.

It is right and instinctive for mothers and expectant mothers to have an overflowing abundance of love and hope in their heart for their child's future and the expectation that they will inherit a state that will provide the necessary support structure and incentives to ensure every Texan reach their maximum potential, young and old alike, for the sake of our state.

The metaphor of a mothers' and an expectant mothers' natural optimism for their child's future is what I harness for the future in all Texans with surety of inheritance because it is essential within a capitalistic system to create enthusiasms that let Texans know that they belong. Always remember, when reading this message, ordinary citizens are absolutely indispensable to everything proclaimed in these writings; the socioeconomic group is insignificant but undeniably useful; emptiness and despair have no barrier. I am a servant of GOD, a watchman by nature, and a romantic with aspirations of being the servant leader of Texas; I intuitively recognize the value of knowledge, wisdom, and the sense of urgency, in which, it must be delivered to all Texans.

I say this with much excitement and yearning for our new future, in my heartfelt, thoughtful pursuit to create something all mothers and Texans can feel safe, secure, and proud about in our communities. So, "do not be disheartened in this pivotal moment in Texas history because this is the time for fresh starts and new beginnings that will elevate our state into a new era."

Texans, sine qua non,
Jack Daniel Foster Jr.

CONTENTS

INTRODUCTION

I am running for the Forward Party-Texas Gubernatorial nomination in 2026, an unprecedented era. Due to Covid-19, in our mist, restraints could possibly be imposed, upon us, so releasing my message in book form will ensure everyone in Texas know my direction and purpose on the record. I want to be clear, I am a thinking man, and other candidates in the nomination process best do the same; this is about a large-scale imagination that provides a vision for stronger communities through the implementation of a well-reasoned, tangible plan to endear our citizens to Texas. Both my heart and mind are with the 254 counties and the thousands of communities that make Texas great, and I will treat every county whether on paper or physically with the utmost respect. All I ask is communities in your county be given the same deference because this is where the root of the problems begin. My deep concern centers around the lives of Texans—rich, middle-class, poor, children, and immigrants—"the quintet". How did we fail to maximize potential and create impoverished conditions, albeit mental or physical?

It would be disingenuous of me not to point out that, constitutionally, the governor of Texas is weak; the authority is shared with the lieutenant governor, and in most cases, the lieutenant governor has concentrated power. I personally don't mind the constitutional power given to the lieutenant governor, but I will be pressing hard for a statewide referendum on the governor's authority to have control of 30 percent of the economic stabilization fund and 30 percent of various agencies' budgets who have no real impact on the lives of Texans. The "30 percent rule" will allow me, as governor, to effectively maneuver in any given situation for the communities of Texas and thwart the lieutenant governor and his cohorts. There are a few more items that I will attach to the referendum and impactful agenda for communities to do their work: appoint both the attorney general and state comptroller of Texas, and create 254 "County Skill Funds" with set funding obligations for counties, along with the creation of "Academic skill funds" in all school districts in the state, with funding obligations also. Each referendum and agenda item has a purpose; it will become evident why I choose these select matters to embody my plan, into the very fabric of each community within Texas.

My governing style will instinctively be proactive; I will focus on the "three determinants of life"—education, health care, and retirement. The impact of the "three determinants" have life-altering consequences, very predictable. The mistakes a person makes in the determinants have tax ramifications that reverberate in all county property and school taxes; this is why it is important to create financial incentives for the individual taxpayer to get involved, not state agencies.

I want to influence our communities to see it from an alternative perspective, my viewpoint, therefore, I call for a new beginning to rebuild both broken and unbroken communities, regain social trust, build new taxpayers through skilled vocational trades, and reward individual taxpayers for investing in their communities, this is twenty-first-century transformational autonomy to impact lives, locally. My uncommon solutions are only uncommon because leaders are conditioned to hold on to traditional governing processes that do not fit this era. They approach problems in a way that fund and task state agencies to do the work of citizens who live in these communities. I will approach problems in a way that allow homeowners, landowners, and buy-in citizens who declare residence, in the county, to pay a fee, exemption for homeowners and landowners, that will use the median property and school taxes in-county to have the right to invest in citizens from communities within their domiciled county, this will be an underlying theme in my message throughout the book. True taxpayers can no longer be left out of a recipe for access and success, in communities within their surrounding area.

Texans, there are two types of taxpayers that exist in our state. "Surface" taxpayers who seem to be disillusioned by the few taxes they do pay, having sales tax added to the price of a good like clothing, cars, furniture, etc., but sales tax can be avoided if nothing is bought. "True" taxpayers cannot simply walk away from the obligatory tax burden of property and school taxes. These obligations require money to be set aside every year from October to January 31 of the new year or fines will ensue, this has always been my concern for the individual taxpayer; there is no property or school tax relief for communities, and no chance of getting any relief. I differ from everyone else, right here, my plan is to create more true taxpayers by giving Texans the ability to recoup their taxes, plus extra, by investing in "social good" for their surrounding communities through public schools, community colleges, life experiences, career planning strategies, mentoring, etc. Ultimately, all communities in Texas become stronger, "true taxpayers", because of one purpose, driven by incentive.

I want to give Texans' insight into how my mind works before moving on to my vision and plan for Texas. There is a question and answer session for the record so you will always be able to check me. Be prepared for critics' attempts to discredit my plan for ordinary Texans, but remember they have offered nothing.

Here is the main scare tactic: he will raise taxes!

Question: Will you increase taxes?

Answer: I have alluded to how a true taxpayer will be able to recoup their tax money, plus extra, earlier in the introduction but "no" to an increase that does not allow for gain through community investment. What you really want to know about is the disconnection between the governor of Texas and the state comptroller of Texas. You see, the governor can give a $25,000 homestead exemption, and the state comptroller can pressure your local appraisal district into negating it through increases in property value, and then the school district backdoors and claims victory with the slogan "No new taxes" on bond issues when they receive more of your money. I want to appoint the state comptroller of Texas because he or she must see the "big picture" and be on the same page as me; lower taxes for all communities across Texas once we build a strong tax base through individual taxpayer investment. Earlier, I wrote that true taxpayers can no longer be left out of a recipe for access and success, in communities within their county. I am committed to building 254 "human capital" investment markets with security for county citizens to always invest in their communities and know it will pay off. Benjamin Franklin once stated, "An investment in knowledge pays the best interest."

Question: Can Jack Daniel Foster Jr. do all the things he talks about for the communities of Texas?

Answer: If I were willing to capitulate my imagination, vision, and plan to state agency, then I would have no choice but to say, "no". But I am not willing to give state agencies the chance to bumble what is rightfully your GOD-given authority, divine right, to do as a resident of both the community and county. I have already mentioned the power of the lieutenant governor in our state, and I have said, "I don't even mind the constitutional power" because my concerns are about ordinary citizens improving their lives through others, responsibly. So I will press for a statewide referendum, allowing the governor authority over 30 percent of the economic stabilization fund and 30 percent of various state agencies' budgets that have little impact on Texans' lives. This will solidify the funds needed to ensure true taxpayers' commitment to their communities through "Skill funds" in every county with the surety of commitment from the state legislature. I am essentially laying the groundwork for communities to always build and prepare for the future. If Texans have power in the present, they will have hope in our new future.

Statement: He is inexperienced, and does not know what he is doing.

Response: In the bible, 1 Corinthians 1:27 states, "But GOD has chosen the simple things of the world to put to shame that which is wise. GOD chose the weak things of the world to put to shame that which is strong."

I guess this is the right statement to make, if you want to avoid dealing with my point of view. To get technical, the Texas Constitution states nothing about experience, creed, ethnicity, religion, etc. to be the governor of Texas. Here is all Texans really need to know: I am a common man, and I always pray and don't lose heart (Luke 18:1), and whatever I do, I honor GOD. You see, to insulate myself from compromising real destiny for the communities across Texas, I must have a statewide referendum—what I talked about in the former question. It seems to me all the experience that these tax collectors have they should make a clean break from traditional governance and do something that will include all the people of Texas. Are they really experienced in the face of hard times? I honestly see it differently, because if they were experienced, they could never let Texans live with the forceable restraints we are expected to live under daily with insecurities—unaffordable postsecondary education, high cost of health care, and minuscule returns on personal savings, not to mention defined contribution accounts associated with employment. I am supposed to be the inexperienced one, yet I am the one talking about increasing your personal funds for savings or recreation. Look around, can you really tell me the "Tax collectors at the statehouse" make your life better? I grade all politicians on how much money I get to keep with services provided and they all get a "F".

Question: What do you think about Black Lives Matter (BLM)?

Answer: I am Texan and African American, and I understand as People of color, we should be able to walk away from an encounter with the police, respectfully with dignity intact. I am totally coherent with the circumstances, which have led to this moment. Always remember this is a governance failure, not a people failure. We operate within a system of governance that gives authority to local associations (i.e., school boards, city councils, county government, community organizations, etc.), so, to get the transformational autonomy all will appreciate, there must be equity spread throughout governance locally. We do this by getting ahead of "tradition" because tradition is what controls change within transformation, thus ebbing the natural flow of inevitable progression; immense weight is placed on these local authorities to hold on to the status quo. I am running for governor of Texas to make all Texans proud of the way I think. Consider this, I will deliberately weaken the local association's chokehold and methodically strengthen the homeowners', landowners', and buy-in citizens' hand to invest in the futures of all citizens from primary and secondary education to community college for skilled vocational trades, bringing people together, amalgamation. The individual taxpayers, who pay property and school taxes or the median of both, will receive an incentive rate for correcting academic deficiencies, ensuring success in relevant skilled trades, and bestowing wisdom. Now this does not preclude anyone from moving on to a traditional four-year college, but it will make a person independent of student loans—only a person with wisdom can give insight into how to do this, or find someone who has this type of experience. We must do it the right way and get understanding because she will serve us all well. Our division on hot-button issues, "barriers and dividers", continue to get in the way of building a prosperous state and nation, so to prove to every Texan that I am worthy to be your governor at this moment, I say to all, "It is time for a new direction. We cannot change the past, but we can construct a future for all to participate." BLM, stay passionate about your issues but do not forget about living (i.e., real income, health care, and saving money). It is about equity, encouraging citizens to right wrongs and do more for those who have been mistreated.

Question: Are you for or against abortion?

Answer: I am a Christian, but I can never tell a woman what to do with their body; therefore, I am for abortion. Texans are probably thinking, *How can you be a Christian and be for abortion?* Let me help you understand why I am a proponent. First, I do not judge a woman's decision concerning her body. Second, we do nothing to help the outlook of both the mother's and child's future. Third, I know of no one who wants to be a mother dependent upon the state to help raise their child. And the final reason is the high probability of never escaping poverty. These reasons, in my humble opinion, are considered conjecture under duress—unfortunately common—when faced with being a parent and no money. This is the moment when a strong community, relative or not, should step to the forefront. The only way to build strong communities and self-esteem, in our people, is to eliminate uncertainty, instability, and any other circumstances that can cause insecurities or poverty; I will empower true taxpaying citizens (i.e., homeowners, landowners, and buy-in citizens) to get involved in the lives of others by providing individual taxpayers with financial incentives, which encourages the guiding hand necessary for stumbles in life, opportunities, and experiences for both advantaged and disadvantaged citizens. When we create an atmosphere of investment in all people, and tangible results are witnessed in all communities, a pregnant woman can now know that she and the unborn child will always have relevance in the present and future. I am trying to rid us of the notion that poverty is forever and move toward the sphere of unlimited opportunity with shared financial benefits, reciprocities.

Question: What is your stand on guns?

Answer: I want to make myself clear before I answer this question. Some battles have no victors; it is causes like these that derail progress in the human condition. Some people are more hell-bent on seeing state gun legislation through to the end more than elevating and preparing people with knowledge and wisdom, which will begin to rid communities of guns and violence to be replaced with hope and enthusiasm, I believe this to be a grave community responsibility; this is another opportunity for individual taxpayers to be incentivized to ensure citizens in their county are knowledgeable about the guns they want to possess or discern their mental state, for possible outreach services. When a true taxpaying citizen is able to invest in fellow citizens for all sorts of skill crafts, licenses, and certifications, a person begins to develop relationships, and they talk, this is when things are laid bare about life, and teaching can begin. I am adamant about twenty-first century transformational autonomy to be focused locally because this is the key to all our social ills. Most problems begin at the local level, but there is no financial incentive for invaluable wisdom to "step-up" and get these problems corrected. The solutions in every county may be very different, but what will be consistent is the economic—financial model, which gives true tax-paying citizens (i.e., homeowners, landowners, and buy-in citizens) empowerment to vest in another citizen's life. To answer the question outright, I am for fingerprint application technology on all guns and law enforcement's judgment.

Question: What is Texas' destiny in your opinion?

Answer: Our destiny will always be intertwined with the past, but we will begin anew, this time, including all Texans favoring no group over another. The focus will be the community, centered around the true taxpayers of Texas (those who pay property and school taxes), but I have added another contributor called the "buy-in citizens." They prefer to rent an apartment or home and so choose to be free of the traditional way of paying the big taxes. The only way a buy-in citizen can invest in citizens in their county is to pay the median property and school tax of that particular county they live. If I am blessed by GOD to be the governor of Texas, it will be the epic moment that seals the faith of twentieth-century governing. We will begin to allow taxpaying citizens to maintain a stake in the future of their community residents through investment in primary and secondary education, trade skills, life experiences (i.e., mentoring, etc.), and enrich individual taxpayers with financial incentives and purpose; we will have found our destiny and change the world. It cannot be emphasized enough, but investment in community residents will always have a risk-free rate attached to ensure the individual taxpayer benefit if any failures should happen. Citizens will recognize tangible benefits accrue to those who pay their property and school taxes, and therefore will aspire to become a taxpaying citizen, so it is important to model these attributes and reward them in all communities across Texas. We will show the other forty-nine states and the world how to repair and reward what really matters—people, rebuilding, and rejuvenating Texas' communities.

Question: How would you deal with environmental issues?

Answer: Let me start by saying, "I am not interested in harming our oil and gas industry, they are the number one contributor to the economic stabilization fund [i.e., rainy day fund], and they put in approximately 85 percent of the money." I am interested in solving our environmental issues through true taxpaying citizens who pay property and school taxes in their county every year. It is important that citizens understand the carbon dioxide problem. We need to eradicate or severely cripple, both gases, carbon dioxide and methane by removing it from our core industries and figure out "free-flowing" or diffusion techniques which can transform these gases into a "philia" for the five atmospheres. Time is running out (i.e., approximately thirty-five to fifty years remaining to solve the problem, so no time to waste); we need all kinds of skilled vocational trades available in every community college across the state to teach welding, diesel and auto mechanics, computer technology, wind turbine technology, aviation mechanics, heating and air-conditioning, water technologies, solar technologies, and all technology courses looking forward—we must have an atmospheric chemistry class specifically pertaining to carbon-methane emissions, to lead thinking minds toward eradication or diffusion-osmotic methodologies. All these skilled vocational trades will be the investment vehicles for true taxpaying citizens— this will tie them to the effort instead of environmental issues being so distant (i.e., homeowner, landowner, and buy-in citizen) and to their benefit through financial incentives by investing in the advantaged and disadvantaged citizens who will benefit professionally, mutual exchange of privileges. The only way this enormous problem gets solved is for all minds and money to have a stake.

As it stands, we do not know who is capable of solving this problem. Is it the common citizen or the PhD in chemistry from the University of Texas? The truth is the human mind is complex, so we must nourish it and see what happens. Alan Turning said it best,

"Sometimes it is the people no one can imagine anything of who do the things no one can imagine." I will take this moment to interject something that seems possibly irrelevant but ties into everything my plan bares out for Texans. We lack the avenues for true taxpayers to feel financial security and relevance for all the taxes they pay, it is like our state government chooses to reward corporations at the expense of communities. The core determinants of life, infrastructure, or structure (i.e., education, health care, and retirement) must be driven through true taxpayers—homeowners, landowners, and buy-in citizens. I am committed to ensuring financial incentives that keep communities perpetually engaged by having both personal and collective prosperity. Never lose sight of my direction and purpose; it is about the defense of dignity and peace for Texans in their communities.

CHAPTER 1

My Vision for Texas:
Our New Future

The true measure of leadership is influence—
nothing more, nothing less.

—21 Irrefutable Laws of Leadership (second law)

In the preamble to the Constitution of the United States, there is only one principle that the state of Texas cannot perform—provide for the common defense. But there is another tenet, last one, that should be emblazoned in every states' sacred economic prowess, "Secure the Blessings of Liberty to ourselves and our Posterity", this is the one salient link that allows Texans to instinctively move toward establishing justice, ensuring domestic tranquility, and promoting the general welfare in their communities, across Texas.

I choose the last tenet, "Secure the Blessings of Liberty to ourselves and our Posterity," as the centerpiece in which my imagination has facilitated a vision that allows for a way to foresee a plan that will perpetually create engagement of all Texans, no matter the ascription or socioeconomic status for the amelioration and amalgamation of our communities and state. Do not let the reference to the Constitution of the United States concern you. Unfortunately, the Texas Constitution does not make any reference yielding to these principles and that is okay, because I will. The key is, I recognize the federal constitution supersedes any state document, depending on stringency, and in this case, my plan for all-out investment in social good within communities across Texas will be justified.

People have a long yearning to contribute to the place they call home, and it is usually their community within their county the desire emerges. As it stands right now, there is no community infrastructure that rewards investment to build on our greatest resource—our fellow Texans. In fact, a perverse incentive exists, which forces us to walk right on by a tragedy that could have been prevented. I know just like you that when there are resources, experience, and wisdom, people tend to follow a real commitment, therefore, we must show strong determination for a newly structured process never before imagined. Regardless of criticism, make people believe in our new future. I want to introduce the concept of twenty-first century transformational autonomy-locally, which encourages real taxpaying citizens to take charge of rebuilding their communities through knowledge and wisdom. When we commit to financial incentives for individual taxpayers, this moment will afford knowledge and wisdom to idle minds for absorption; the positive effect of these efforts will be far beyond what we can predict, for the quintet.

No one will be excluded from the individual taxpaying citizen's grasp (i.e., homeowner, landowner, and buy-in citizen). Persons who rent an apartment or home must pay the median property and school tax in the county they reside for rights and privileges to invest in community citizens, primary and secondary education, skilled vocational trades, life experiences, seminar opportunities, and any other social good that improves lives. The criteria for investees is wide because it is meant to include everyone—advantaged and disadvantaged citizens. The only difference is the higher incentive rate, it is designed to encourage an investor to pursue a disadvantaged citizen with just as much zeal as an advantaged citizen. And the added bonus—if anyone fails, the investor will always have a risk-free rate. I never want the pursuit of knowledge and wisdom to not be rewarded. Every endeavor between the investors and investees are creating the interactions that bring communities closer to their common purpose we are trying to build across Texas, in which every Texan has a stake in our new future—social trust.

My vision and plan for Texas goes straight to the heart of all the socioeconomic problems we have in our communities. Everything good has a social component to it, hence, "Social good" should flow through the greatest state government support system—individual taxpaying citizens. Only a person who pays property and school taxes will understand what I am talking about; it is extremely frustrating to throw good money away—meaning, there is never a return on investment either in citizenry or money, (i.e., taxes mandated to pay every year). And if you do not watch-out taxes will increase, it is a constant battle. The good part about this issue is no matter the political persuasion, homeowners and landowners are connected to it, and for inclusionary purposes, the category I call "buy-in citizens" will be considered to share the burden also because they will have to pay the median property and school taxes within their county to have the designation county investor.

These taxpaying citizens are not mere mortals to our state but treated as such. I do not distinguish between the sizes of homes, amount of land, etc. The point is that property and school taxes are being paid, so my attention is focused on creating a way to elevate real tax obligations and dedication to community, county, and state, right order, versus the small contributions of "sales tax and state assistance"—no endearment to Texas. And throughout the year, there are tax-free days. I know people try to shield their kids from harsh truths—property and school taxes—as they grow up, but this harsh and hidden truth must be explained to all who aspire to have stability. I want it out in the open with tangible benefits accruing to "community servants" who choose to invest in our most prized assets-county citizenry. It should be instinctive to help people improve their lives through all legitimate means, this is the tragedy of twentieth-century governance—it allows free-will without guidance. There is no sanctity in environments of ignorance. These types of perpetuations put undue burdens on homeowners, landowners, and buy-in citizens by ultimately increasing taxes.

My vision for Texas is not only for true taxpayers to know they are appreciated, but it also has a plan that supports the vision. The plan allows communities to target specific troubles: substance abuse, gangs, gun violence, and suicides if necessary. I am trying to get us as close to our "perfect purpose" as possible. Texans must see clearly that our social and economic calamities have no color barrier, political persuasion, or financial protections. We are all susceptible, so it behooves us to have a structured system in place where all communities can use a creative transformational process to beat societal woes.

I foresee homeowners, landowners, and buy-in citizens leading the effort to ensure stability through knowledge in primary-secondary education and skilled vocational trades that lead to certifications, licensures, and all kinds of technical fields unforeseen. This will allow the individual taxpayer to benefit financially from their investment (i.e., tuition, books, mentoring, tutoring, building strong communities, confidence, trust, and hope in the future). The front-end personal investments will yield important tangible results that imprint citizens for life because this is not just a "money" investment, the personal talks, experiences and priceless wisdom imparted; there is no quantitative figure for these interactions. I want citizens to love their community, county, and state. I want every Texan to be proud and know Texas has your communities' back.

We have yet to reach our zenith, because of the failure to use our full imagination; we must use money as a means to an end. Our aim should always be to provide financial incentives to stimulate interaction among communities to create hope and posterity, which leads to personal and collective prosperity. The purpose of this plan is not to make money, though, I want homeowners, landowners, and buy-in citizens to make all they can but meet the needs in their community, responsibly.

In my opinion, some of the greatest legislation like the Square Deal, the New Deal, Social Security, Medicare, the Great Society, and the GI Bill all lacked governors, past and present, who failed to incorporate the essence of these federal laws into state legislation. The essence is the protection of citizens (i.e., at the county, state, and federal level) that extend from the lower to the upper level, but this never happens correspondingly. This is why I will be seeking a state-wide referendum on the power of the governorship—seeking a 30 percent rule for accessing the economic stabilization fund (i.e., rainy day fund) and agencies' budgets that have no real impact on ordinary citizens' lives. This moment in time cries out for new leadership and creative state legislation that will secure real financial securities to promote community investment.

Our new future is a vision and plan that encompasses a number of aims. Consequently, the state legislation will be called the "big deal." The implementation will give the governor unprecedented funding mechanisms: create skill funds in all counties for adult investment, which will use the concept of "public-controlled capitalism"; create an academic skills fund for school districts that are to follow the same concept as the county skills fund; create a Community Protection Commission to safeguard the county skills fund in every county, with compensation; renewed commitment to broadband construction throughout the state; appoint the state's attorney general and comptroller, both will be part of the state-wide referendum.

The big deal state legislation will commit to every Texans' preparation and security. The true taxpayers who pay property and school taxes will be given the right to invest in school-age students through high school and adulthood to build their futures tirelessly, obtaining financial incentives for themselves so to fund personal recreation, retirement funding, health-care savings, etc., giving the true taxpayer a well-deserved sense of security and pertinence while preparing the next generation to do and live responsibly. The duties individual taxpayers are being tasked to do for the good of community are grave, consequential, and pivotal in societal maturation, thus, worthy of financial incentive. This is not the job for state agencies. It is right to be placed in the hands of the individual taxpayer.

This state legislation (the big deal) will move aggressively toward cementing affordability in health care for all Texans by negotiating hospital expansions, supply side, and expanding Medicaid temporarily with a higher-income threshold and gradually eliminating as community investment prepare citizens for skilled labor job markets, joint hospital cooperation agreements between counties, eliminate state insurance commissioner discretions on health insurance issues, and ask for a serious sit-down with the big health-care insurance corporations. The main reason I would like to talk with the health insurance corporations is that I honestly want to know what their real concerns are for health-care cost in the future. How can the state of Texas get the price of health insurance premiums monthly per category to young adults, $50; mid-adults, $100; and families, $150? We are dealing with private health insurance, not government. I will also be applying for a CMS waiver for Texas seniors as we come online with different health-care policies. Depending on the answers I receive from the big health insurance corporations, I will adjust the health-care initiatives formerly mentioned and go in the direction that leads to monthly health insurance premiums being around the categories listed for young adults, mid-adults, and families. It is critically important that citizens in Texas be able to afford monthly premiums with ease to take care of their own health-care needs and feel secure, some citizens need to be prepared for this necessary social good. If elected governor, it will be a priority for constant public service announcements with celebrity Texans about health insurance and unnecessary ER visits.

Keep in mind that every action taken is to give Texans more money, freedom, and security to begin anew in their community and make it strong with investment in knowledge for neighborhood opportunities, and wise advice; bind yourself up into whoever you choose to invest your money, effort, and time because I expect responsible Texans to be imitated across this great state. When ordinary Texans are given a seat at "their table" to take care of their community, and the governor provides the necessary tools with consequential funding along with a full state legislature commitment to the big deal, this will create the necessary security for individual taxpaying citizens to continuously prepare community citizenry for the ultimate prize, $15 to $30 trillion plus, exporting to the world carbon dioxide-methane eradication or diffusion-osmotic methodologies for exhaustive gases, cement, chemicals, air-conditioning, electrical and water technologies, etc. There are no limits in a state that invest in all the necessary infrastructure for citizens to thrive—

primary, secondary, and postsecondary skilled education—to reach maximum zenith in all Texans.

Let me make sure that everyone understands, I have nothing against traditional four-year college education. I am about making sure everyone has the capacity to live and always improve themselves without a four-year college degree, because it is the skilled vocational trades that initially return more on investment. I think it to be wise to get a skilled vocational trade through an individual taxpayer first, then if a person chooses to go to a traditional college, it will be more affordable without student loans. Sometimes, life can get in the way of college, and some never make it back. And it is a real shame to not finish college and continue to have a student loan to contend with. My way eliminates the hassle of student loans by allowing individual taxpayers to invest in a person for a skilled vocational trade at a community college that will lead to a certification or licensure and an associate degree with the basics transferring and, of course, the homeowner, landowner, or buy-in citizen obtaining financial incentives to ensure success.

The big deal legislation does not address retirement plans directly because it is the jurisdiction of the US Department of Labor and its regulatory boards; community investment is outside their regulatory authority. Unfortunately, there is no way for Texans to add the proceeds of community investment to retirement plans such as DC's 401(k), 403(b), 457(b), SERP, and IRAs connected to retirement plans and DB's pension plans. But if you are a business owner, it can be done or go to a retail broker. The point is, Texans, there will be no lack of options for your money—more disposable income, reinvest in community, another brokerage account, increase recreation time, etc. In my mind, the lack of options is directly correlated with not providing options to increase well-being, quality of life, the standard of living, reaching personal goals, or helping others reach theirs. In other words, if options (i.e., ideas, plans) for the betterment of life are intentionally limited, then Texans can never maximize their full unenumerated might within amendments 9 and 10 in the Bill of Rights, powerful additions to the US Constitution.

The Big Deal's Purpose

Personal security-conceptualized

The big deal's legislation is simplistic and guided by individual taxpayer's security in the community economy. The state and county governments will deal with making health care affordable through the health-care initiatives referred to earlier. Three critical components are left in the hands of our homeowners, landowners, and buy-in citizens, (i.e., true taxpayers): invest in their communities' primary-secondary education, skilled vocational trades, and other supports that may be necessary for success. And, of course, enjoy the financial incentives for retirement or recreation from investment in county citizenry.

There should be no confusion about who we want our citizens to admire in my vision and plan for Texas. The big deal's legislation will allow the governor to share power with communities across our great state to ensure the necessary reach to all citizens. Normally, money channels from state to county governments to distribute as they see fit, and this is where everything tends to go wrong because some Commissioners' courts will sabotage anything they do not believe in or a friend cannot get a contract out of. Not this time, Dillon's Rule will be modified, the money will go into a "skills fund" in every county in the state, totally separate from the county budget with its own accounting to be maintained by the county treasurer and county clerk to work closely with the Community Protection Commission. Rural counties will be expected to contribute $2 million every two years but could increase depending on the "skills fund" depletion rate. Urban counties will be expected to fund at a rate of $5 million per million of population every two years—maybe higher depending on fund depletion rate. And the state of Texas will contribute approximately eleven to fifteen million to every county skills fund every legislative year. Remember, I talked about the statewide referendum on the governor's power and authority to use 30 percent of the economic stabilization fund and state agencies' budgets, deemed not impactful on the lives of Texans. I want to ensure that opportunities for investment in community citizenry is always the right thing to do, and individual taxpayers will be rewarded for it.

Every community college in the state of Texas will be viewed as the investment vehicle of first choice, for individual taxpayers, so students will have no interest in using financial aid, only cash for tuition, books, tutoring, mentoring, computers, etc. I expect community colleges to acquire the latest skilled technologies and design the best programs to build a twenty-first-century workforce. The expectations are no independent "stand-alone" programs without affiliation with a community college because true taxpayers can only get financial incentives by investing in skilled vocational trades for certifications, licensures, and associate degrees in community colleges with the ability to transfer credits upon the decision to apply to a traditional four-year college. So, there should be no funding issues when money intentionally flows through community colleges for the amelioration of communities and individual taxpayers.

All of us are part of the US economy, but our lives unfold in the Texas economy, nevertheless that does not mean protections cannot be built into communities, guaranteeing individual taxpayers the right to invest their money in community citizens and citizens having the right to improve their lives, continuously. The constant ability to improve one's technical skills for the job market is what the last tenet in the preamble of the United States Constitution is all about: "Secure the blessings of liberty to ourselves and our posterity."

The big deal will eradicate the traditional business cycles' life disruptions and mitigate the oil and gas boom-and-bust recurring sequences through the stewards of community (i.e., true taxpayers). It will be vitally important that unemployment be defeated with the constant diversification of careers. I should also say, "an individual taxpayer can invest in themselves and others, simultaneously, for new skilled vocational trades, licensures, certifications, and associate degrees." Right now, the governor, lieutenant governor, and state legislators, i.e., tax collectors, will take these situations as an undefeatable circumstance and throw money at the situation, temporarily, until the next time. All these situations of unemployment are dealt with through state agencies, and this is where Texans should see the difference between my vision and plan to divert monies in the direction of individual taxpayers instead of state bureaucracy and paperwork. Give yourself a chance to do what is right, your divine right.

The situations and circumstances that develop over time in the lives of Texans, such as unemployment, isolation, desolation, drug use, home evictions, crime, prison, homelessness, and overall instability and insecurity, I call dismal infinity. First, it can be corrected only one way—time spent with experienced Texans. Dismal infinity is a perpetual financial trap that can give glimpses of financial hope but encapsulates people in the spiral of ups and downs related to the job market and causes low morale, which makes people vulnerable to all sorts of things, particularly hate groups.

Dismal infinity

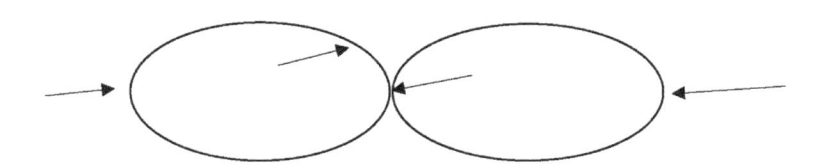

It does not matter the starting point in dismal infinity; place the dot anywhere, bottom, top, left, right, middle, curves on either side, but make sure the starting point, i.e., finger or trace point is also the ending point as the loop is followed. What will be found out is, no matter the starting point, there is no immunity from vulnerabilities (i.e., middle class and marginalized citizens). The ups and downs of the business cycles, oil and gas, and the overall Texas economy can be mitigated or rendered irrelevant as the big deal's legislation shields our communities and protects individual taxpayers to do their good works.

There are too many life-altering aspects, dismal infinity, in our lives to let the natural economic course, ups and downs, inflect nonsensical damage on capable Texans, who just need an injection of hope from their community. Repair communities through investment in primary and secondary education, skilled vocational trades, and the necessary supports for real success in local and state economy, so to protect and reward individual taxpayers for giving of their time and effort to such a noble cause—to bless others. The father of conservatism, Edmund Burke, states, "A state without the capacity for some change is a state without its means of conservatism. Sometimes the dead must be overruled." So if there continues to be no room for the improvement of citizens' lives and nothing for taxpayers to benefit from besides the stock market, conservation will be over with shortly. The irony is that I will save conservatism with the big deal's legislation by ensuring taxpaying citizens are able to invest their money in community and obtain respectable financial incentives and returns, so citizens will be prepared to pay their fair share.

Economic protection

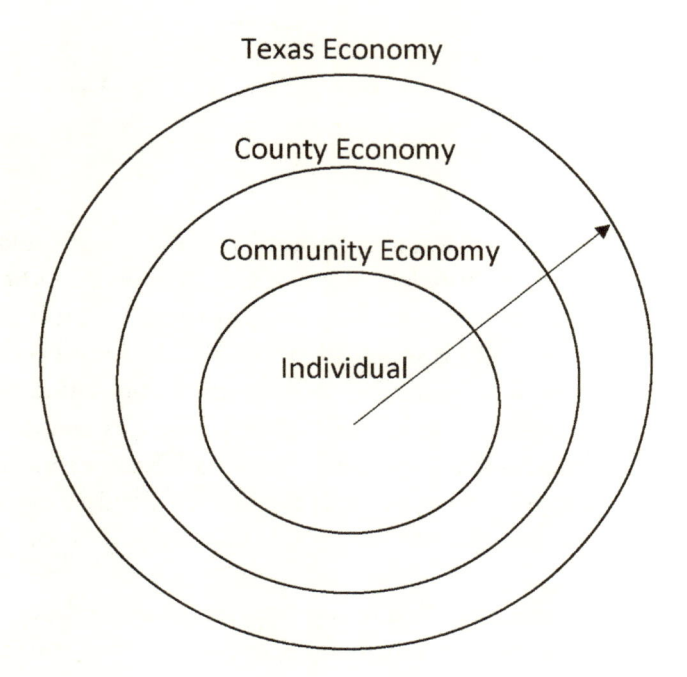

Texas Economy

County Economy

Community Economy

Individual

The individual is the ultimate contributor to Texas, the county, and the community economy. An individual must be prepared in every community throughout the state to successfully move through all layers of the economy to take on their role as a true taxpaying citizen. The individual will be protected from the other two layers of economy, Texas and County, by community—with investment in the latest skilled vocational trades and necessary supports to ulti-mately become a contributor at all levels without protection. To do it right, the necessary guidance may take up to three years, the individ-ual taxpayer will receive respectable financial returns all three years for their investment, plus principal. This is all about rewarding posi-tive externalities, social good and social trust, to fill communities up with hope and the tangibles for a bright future.

A striking picture should be emerging for my vision and plan for Texans; a dual purpose in communities across Texas, which will empower people and foster a real sense of working toward individual security. As we know, all things work together for good to those who love GOD and to those who are called according to His purpose (Romans 8:28). I will never stop honoring GOD in what I see for the land we all love. When all the parts are put together that matter—people, incentives, education, health care, retirement, and the environment—we will excel and do unimaginable things that will benefit every Texan.

CHAPTER 2

Public Controlled Capitalism

Only secure leaders give power to others.
—*21 Irrefutable Laws of Leadership* (twelfth law)

I refer to our economic system as Babylonian capitalism because of the harsh way citizens in our country are dealt with in the three determinants of life (i.e., education, health care, and retirement), which infer great insight as to how a person's life will unfold, due to a lack of life infrastructure preparation. I do not indict our economic system but render strong disapproval with hope to its hubris, selfishness, self-centeredness, thievery, and depravity. The criticisms levied are only to make it better as we move toward twenty-first-century governance, in Texas, this is why it is an imperative that the focus be placed on communities. There are absolutely no reasons an impenetrable sphere cannot be placed around every community in Texas to operate as a certainty within a county rather than an uncertainty.

The big deal's legislation will use the concept of public-controlled capitalism, which assigns incentive rates for two categories of citizens (i.e., advantaged and disadvantaged citizens) and a risk-free rate, all to encourage individual taxpayers' investment in local citizenry for social good (i.e., primary-secondary education, skilled vocational trades, certifications, associate degree, etc.) upon creation of a county skills fund and academic-skills fund in every county and independent school district across the state. The "intellectual product" should not be mistaken for state-controlled capitalism because this idea essentially places Texans' money in the states' hand to be used by the state bureaucracy, which is no good for the individual taxpayer.

Public-controlled capitalism is meant to work in the communities' favor by allowing homeowners, landowners, and buy-in citizens the irresistible chance to enhance their wealth and simultaneously improve the lives of others in all communities within their county boundaries by separating these unique structured opportunities from national, state, and county economies. Isolating the community economy, using public controlled capitalism, from the other three economies produces a "synergistic latitude" that will generate the knowledge expansion that gives individual taxpayers the foundation and capabilities to solve our most damming issue—poverty. The bigger the economy- county, state, or national, the greater the inefficiencies in combating negative externalities such as lack of educational opportunities, unaffordable health care, and no real support structure to aid in a successful transition, in any part of the economy.

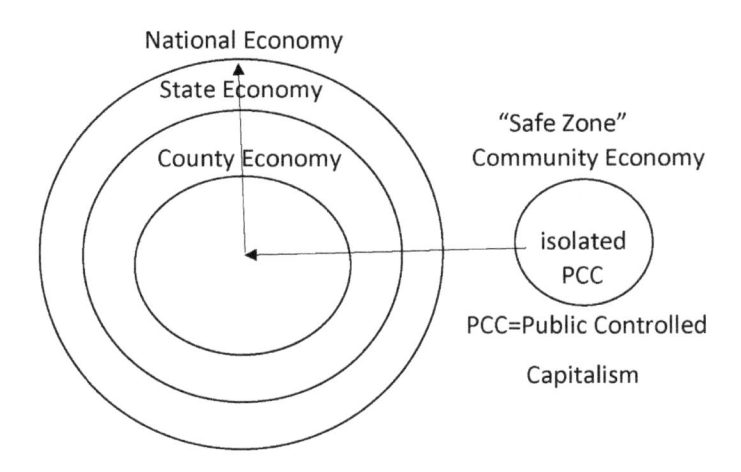

Twenty-first century transformational autonomy at the county level focused on communities coupled with the incentive-based public-controlled capitalistic concept will give true taxpayers, those who pay property and school taxes, the full authority to invest, i.e., plenipotentiary, in county citizenry, in communities, throughout the county preparing townsman for entry into the county, state, and national economies. The thorough process by way of individual tax-payers will take time and effort in rebuilding our communities, the right way, in conjunction with community colleges in Texas, which will provide relevant skilled vocational trades, and true taxpayers will do the rest with financial incentives.

The future of Texas cannot be left up to families alone because too much is at stake, now; families are under serious financial con-straints, advantaged and disadvantaged, and to deprive our state of its very own natural talent is an abomination. We do not know the value of our intellectual talent spread out across this great state and the incredible foreknowing they may have stored within themselves, these are our communities—rich, poor, middle class, black, white, brown, etc. The best wisdom is not a matter of analysis or princi-ple, it flows directly from the heart. Texans, what I am talking about cannot be captured with standardized tests and may not be shown in a person's attire or personality; it is realized only when an experi-enced person is willing to give time and effort to break through all the facades and unlock what is, really, inside another. The illogical reasoning of letting people do it themselves (i.e., free-will, stumbling through life until a possible career break comes along) is a nonsensi-cal tax giveaway in my opinion because that person could have been influenced to go to a community college and obtain several skilled vocational trades in high demand, courtesy of an individual taxpayer who pay property and school taxes. And the individual taxpayer will receive a financial incentive for the advantaged or disadvantaged citi-zen upon successful completion of the skilled trade with certification or licensure, or receive the risk-free rate if failure should happen. The whole point is to coach them through to the end of the journey. Not all people are strong in the face of adversity, but seasoned Texans can show their county citizenry how to whether the toils and snares of life.

The tax burden will only get higher and higher at the county level (i.e., property and school taxes) if we fail to act in a manner that will prevent divestment in communities across Texas. We must sufficiently satisfy individual taxpayers and comparably give our county citizens, both advantaged and disadvantaged, purpose, which will inspire hope for a new beginning. In 2018, the Bureau of Census Research found that poverty had increased in Texas by 33 percent, approximately eighty-four counties locked in hopelessness because there is no plan to undo the damage done by our state bureaucracy. At this moment in our state, we continue to feed the cycle of poverty with welfare checks, Medicaid, housing assistance, utility assistance, etc., anything to keep people dependent on the system. Public-controlled capitalism will shine brighter in dire circumstances more so than any other prevalence because it is meant to give people a reason to look out for one another. We know all the wrong actions have been taken time and time again because the manifestation of desperation is always the same in every generation: a sheer longing to do better, take care of family, contribute in a positive way to society, earn a decent living, have a nice house, affordable health care, good retirement, etc. Our state has systematically stripped hope away from a lot of Texans, and I aim to give us all abundant redemption.

I never want to be perceived as downplaying the importance of money in my plan. It is a real motivator that can be directed to do good for every community that constitutes our 254 counties, which ultimately bring Texas into existence. The goal is not to make money but to meet the needs of every Texan and help our citizens understand our lives center around the three determinants of life—education, health care, and retirement. Under my imagination, vision, and plan, perpetual preparation is key, so it must begin with the most experienced citizens within communities who are homeowners, landowners, or buy-in citizens. These are the citizens committed to the state of Texas, therefore, it is a necessity to reward them with financial incentives to impart wisdom and invest in their community.

The concept of public-controlled capitalism will propel educational learning in both independent school districts and community colleges without student loans, FAFSA, or grants by allowing individual taxpayers to invest in their communities and receive an 8 percent incentive rate for a disadvantaged citizen who successfully completed a skilled vocational trade program, a 5 percent incentive rate for an advantaged citizen that successfully completed a skilled vocational trade program, and a 3 percent incentive rate (risk-free) for either advantaged or disadvantaged citizens who fail to successfully complete a skilled program. Every individual taxpayer must pay their property and school taxes completely, and creative deals can also be made with other homeowners, landowners, or buy-in citizens. Every individual taxpayer is limited to three citizens, i.e., maximum six with creative deals, in their county to ensure quality and no monopolies. All community colleges across the state are eligible for county citizenry education if the skilled vocational trade is not offered in the local area. Incentive rates are only given for community colleges, no stand-alone schools, and reimbursements for tutoring and mentoring while dining, books, tuition, are all factored into the incentive rate received for the investee and make sure to keep all receipts for validation purposes. The incentive rate will be paid no earlier than a year and a day or upon the county citizen's completion of the skilled vocational trade program.

Individual taxpayers will be rewarded in an extraordinary manner by receiving all principal or expenditures in addition to the incentive rate, cash or check, by the Community Protection Commission in their domiciled county after verification of the investee's successful completion or failure. We need a process of repairing and rewarding, both advantaged and disadvantaged citizens, to believe that everyone will mutually benefit naturally in their community. There should not be any struggle when capable people are around to lend a helping hand for the improvement of life; this creates both personal and collective prosperity.

The financial incentive rates embedded in public-controlled capitalism serves to reinforce the desired response that causes Texans to pursue family and neighbors within the community and other citizens throughout the county, who may possibly be in unfamiliar areas of the county, for skilled vocational trade programs; this is important and tangible to all of Texas because it allows for the stubbornly persistent reach of our new state government to impact all lives the right way through individual taxpayers in their community. There is nothing, I believe, that cannot equip a citizen for a responsible life, in paying taxes, lifelong commitment to education, affordable health care, and retirement savings, than a caring and concerned community.

I will forever have an empire state of mind about Texas. We can save the world right here in our state with new inventions, technologies, techniques, methods, etc. by investing in our communities, not corporations. I am not concerned about currying favor with any corporation because of the unbridled intellect Texas communities will begin unleashing upon the world, more corporations will inevitably be created. This means creative destruction could be at hand for corporations that refuse to embrace this moment, and new corporations will have the mindset in Texas that community investment is priority number one, not tax breaks, subsidies, and county abatements to companies. The goal is twenty to fifty billion in education over four years to true taxpayers, creating an environment of investment in human capital (i.e., county citizenry) for strong academic foundations and skilled vocational trades, certifications, licensures, and beyond. My eye is on capturing $15 to $30 trillion from the world in tropospheric cleaning technologies for exhaustive gases, chemicals, cement, electricity, air-conditioning, and atmospheric-dissipating carbon dioxide-methane methodologies. The pathway will be set for the world to follow: a county skills fund and academic skills fund to reward individual taxpaying citizens; community investment to encourage skilled vocational trades before traditional college, and instilled responsibility towards continuing education, health care, retirement savings, and devotion to community, i.e., property and school taxes.

We cannot end poverty, until we figure out how to eliminate greed—my plan, but we can make it our mission to defeat both poverty and greed in Texas; through public-controlled capitalism, we defy stoicism (i.e., racism, prejudice, homophobia, elitism, hate groups, etc.) and status quo governing by giving a commitment to all Texans, no selected groups. Every Texan will be assigned a classification (advantaged or disadvantaged citizen) and an incentive rate to coincide with the designation: advantaged—5 percent, disadvantaged—8 percent. And whosoever chooses to invest in their county citizenry for skilled vocational trades and necessary support structures will never lose money because of the risk-free rate—3 percent. I only hope as people read the words on these pages their imagination may spring forth, asking themselves, *Where would I be if public-controlled capitalism had been in place?* The concept itself is to establish justice, ensure domestic tranquility, promote the general welfare, and "secure the Blessings of Liberty to ourselves and our Posterity" (preamble of the United States Constitution). There is no precedent for application of the economic-financial portions of the big deal's legislation; it is Texans helping Texans, with incentives, state history in the making with serious significance for the world.

The burdens, problems, and pressures of life have been made to be unbearable now, even though most struggle knowing one false move could mean financial disaster. I say to myself, *How can our state-elected officials claim to love Texas and let this happen to Texans?* The real mistake is putting people in "high places" who have no connection to the throes of life; a person who has not lived among ordinary people is less likely to understand how common people think and what they need. Texans, we need to elect thinkers who have the ability to make decisions based on fairness, elect thinkers that will constantly look out for those who have not had an adequate opportunity because of individuals or institutions who have robbed people, devalued people, and demeaned people, in some way, elect thinkers who will not add any extra burden to people who already have a hard time, whether it be immigrants, children, or the marginalized, and elect thinkers who will not harm people just because state power informally consents, benign neglect (Jeremiah 22:1–5). All these instructions must always be at the forefront of a decision maker's thought process. I believe wholeheartedly that when Texans are given the power to bestow their wisdom upon fellow citizens and receive financial incentives for improving lives in their community, we will be closer and closer to GOD's designed purpose for life.

When things are at their worst we must go inward, believing in community where we choose to live, to make our economic and financial circumstances better. It is state government that unfortunately makes things worse because they are literally out of touch with both rural and urban ways of life. State agencies or bureaucrats do not work for Texans, they work to stymie progress, ensure dependence, and keep themselves irrelevant in our minds. It is this Kafkaesque vagary that twists peoples' thinking about how all levels of government work, and it is actually successful in causing people to give up altogether, yet Texans keep paying their property and school taxes as they get higher and higher, hoping for a better day. Here is a perfect example: the General Land Office received a billion dollars from the federal government to rebuild homes for Texans who were devastated during hurricane Harvey. To date, they have rebuilt approximately two thousand homes. What happens when another hurricane comes barreling in? Do we let state bureaucracy start over wasting money again? I guess we can call this "government at work" seeming relevant but not an effective use of our tax dollars. If the state is involved in rebuilding homes, it means something is amiss. For example, people receiving help from the state did not have the requisite insurance, living from paycheck to paycheck, no health insurance, etc. Why would state bureaucracy permit such a thing to happen when people are ill-equipped to handle themselves, let alone a house? They keep setting citizens up for failure, and of course, they fall for it because everyone wants a house, right?

I mentioned earlier the statewide referendum on the power of the governorship and the 30 percent rule for bureaucracy such as the General Land Office. I want to take 30 percent of any state agencies' budget that do not impact lives and redistribute it to the "skills fund" in all 254 counties. There are so many necessary support structures that must be in place for communities to thrive and for true taxpayers to impart their knowledge and wisdom, but Texans must be paid to do "good works" in their community, just as state agency employees. I am emphatic and passionate about giving homeowners, landowners, and buy-in citizens their right to be filled with pride building their savings up and having a big role in developing individual talent, social trust, and credibility at home in their community; this is what will make public-controlled capitalism work, i.e., amelioration and amalgamation.

Do not be afraid of the new role I want to hoist onto your shoulders, it was always meant to be this way, but traditional governance would lead a person to think otherwise. I remain steadfast in what I see for all Texans—rich, middle class, marginalized citizens, children, and immigrants. We only get to the "not yet" together and supply the lack of each other. At a moment like this, it will take a state leader who can elevate the governorship beyond the possible and catapult it into the impossible; this is empowerment with direction and purpose for communities all over Texas.

Sometimes, our leaders can have incredible knowledge but irrelevant when it comes to Texans' lives. We know this to be true because community colleges are unaffordable to most Texans, and health care is too expensive, alongside leading the nation in uninsured citizens and no possible way to earn respectable returns outside of Wall Street. Why does it have to be like this? Some say that "this is the way it is." No, I refuse to accept costs that determine outcomes, such as quality of life, standard of living, and state of being, Texans will have to endure for a lifetime. Have you ever drove past a run-down apartment complex and wondered, "How do they make it?" Do you know any young or older adults who have no direction or someone full of potential and intellect but no money? Do you know of any school-age children, primary or secondary, who need tutoring after school, one-on-one? These questions are community-based and can only be solved locally with financial incentives to homeowners, landowners, and buy-in citizens. Every social good we know that stabilizes, encourages, and gives hope to people requires a financial component to allow follow-through with time, effort, money, and individual wisdom. Texans, community rebuilding has nothing to do with benevolence; it cannot be free when everyone has light bills, water bills, mortgages, car notes, grocery bills, health care, retirement savings, etc. State bureaucracy will never be as efficient as individual Texans taking care of their communities; this is why if I am elected as your governor, I will be secured with confidence in sharing power and money with Texans to impact the lives of others.

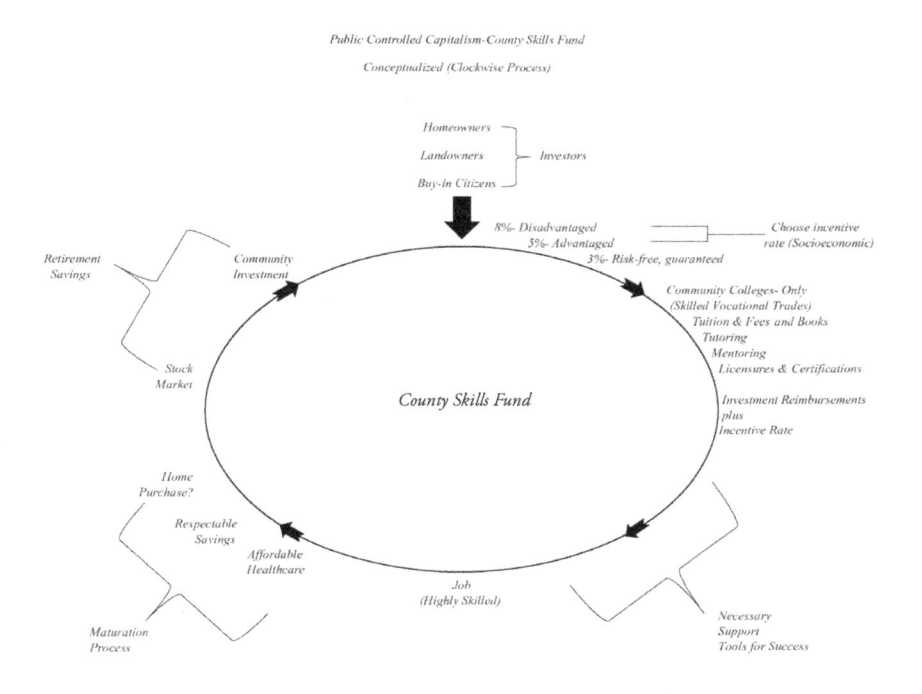

Explanation to follow the diagram.

Public-Controlled Capitalism: County Skills Fund

One of the major aims of the big deal state legislation is to encourage and create vehement pursuit of county citizenry for legitimate technical skills with certifications and licensures, giving everyone a head start in life, whether advantaged or disadvantaged citizens. Financial aid and student loans will be discouraged at the community college level because public-controlled capitalism is designed specifically for community taxpaying citizens to invest in their county citizenry to supplement income for recreation, traditional savings, and retirement plans associated with employment, allowing homeowners, landowners, and buy-in citizens to do the real work for social good in their communities with economic and financial interest (i.e., equity).

Every county will have a "skills fund," which will operate under the concept of public-controlled capitalism, conceptualized in a clockwise process. The diagram above depicts the general flow of how we will repair and reward Texas communities and individual taxpaying citizens across our great state.

(I should also note in the diagram not shown is the Community Protection Commission, which will be located in every county. They will be responsible for payment of the incentive rates, reimbursements, verification of investment in citizenry, and validations from beginning to end and assisted with accounting by the county treasurer and county clerk.)

Homeowners, landowners, and buy-in citizens

At the very top of the illustration, there are three distinct investors: homeowners, landowners, and buy-in citizens. Homeowners and landowners have automatic privileges to invest in local citizens and prisoners, housed in Texas Department of Criminal Justice institutions, across the state because they pay property and school taxes. Buy-in citizenry, non-owners or renters, can pay the median tax in property and school taxes in their domiciled county to reserve the right to invest in county citizenry and prisoners throughout the state. All taxes must be paid by January 31.

Incentive rates

The homeowner, landowner, and buy-in citizen can pursue advantaged or disadvantaged citizens only three at a time, i.e., six with creative deals, for skilled vocational trades, but receiving the highest incentive rate of 8 percent is reserved for the most vulnerable in communities because it is extremely important we have inclusion of all Texans. Investment in county citizens will include the principal (i.e., expenditures on tuition, fees, and books) along with possible tutoring, mentoring, certification, and licensure examination. Upon successful completion, reimbursement of expenditures in addition to incentive rate will be awarded.

Risk-free rate

The risk-free rate is for either advantaged or disadvantaged citizens (i.e., investees for skilled vocational trades). If failure should occur in any skilled programs for whatever reason, the investor can cash out and receive payment of expenditures plus 3 percent. We are sending two signals: do not give up on your community, and every Texan is a valued citizen, advantaged or disadvantaged. There is absolutely no reason why every citizen in our state cannot be prepared to be a true taxpaying citizen, courtesy of homeowners, landowners, and buy-in citizenry within their county.

Community colleges

The essential life-altering work that must be done will be placed in the hands of our community colleges across the state for all the technical skills at present and in the future. These "breadbaskets" will save us by putting a strong emphasis on water technologies, carbon dioxide emission eradication technologies in exhaustive gases, air-conditioning, cement, electricity, and atmospheric technologies. And with financing from individual taxpayers through their cash payments for citizens to obtain skilled vocational trades, there are endless possibilities to what will be occurring in our community colleges. Because of what is at stake, all stand-alone technical schools must be affiliated with a community college in Texas, or individual taxpayer investors will not obtain reimbursement plus incentive rate. Stand-alone technical schools have a serious problem with stability, and their financial model depends on student loans and grant amounts from the government, thus, putting valuable future technical skills at risk.

Necessary support tools

The elapse of time (i.e., the blank space) is where I hope mentoring facilitates a valued friendship that can be everlasting despite investment completion. The necessary support tools are in the hands of the investor. Community colleges are great institutions of learning but do not teach wisdom, these are the moments where insight into responsible living can occur. To build a great society we must pay for it, therefore, I must reward the citizens who have labored long and hard for what they have obtained in life and encourage them in every way to bestow all the knowledge and life experiences possible in our communities. I depend heavily upon the experienced in our society to do what the federal, state, and county governments can Never do, unite us—amalgamation.

Jobs—highly skilled

Life is transformed with hope and promise at this point in the diagram, but I need the investor (i.e., individual taxpayer) to be ever-present for guidance with experience, knowledge, and wisdom despite the completion of a skilled vocational trade program because responsibilities must be realized—continuing education in skills, health-care insurance, disposable and retirement savings, etc.

Maturation process

Go back to the beginning of the diagram and think about what it will take for a person to get this far in life without the guidance of the experienced and their wisdom. We put our citizens and communities fifteen to twenty years into stability instead of instability with front-end investment in skilled vocational trades and the necessary support tools. Mentoring and support structures during and after the investment phase will place Texans in an equipped position to handle all the important responsibilities that Texas expects of every citizen.

Public-controlled capitalism will be more than just an investment regimen for homeowners, landowners, and buy-in citizens; it methodically builds personal and collective prosperity for all Texans through equity, which will cause Texans to have concern for one another's interest. The canons will be looking to add to their bank accounts by investing in county citizenry for technical skills while the investee will be yearning to improve their quality of life, tangible progression, as that process evolves. Mentoring and friendships develop that segue to responsible living that will entail talks about having health insurance, respectable savings, and potentially purchasing a home, etc.

Retirement savings

The stock market is only accessible in two ways to working and retired citizens, either through retail investing or retirement plans associated with places of employment. Both are legitimate means of making money in the future to secure a "three- or four-legged stool" of comfort in a successful retirement: private savings, retirement plan savings; social security; and possibly a traditional IRA, Roth IRA, SERP, or Keogh—but takes thirty to forty years to develop.

Investment tools, such as the county skills fund and academic skills fund, will be the instruments to supplement private savings and give Texans more choice in what to do with extra money, options like re-investing only in county citizenry for skilled vocational trades, or both re-investing in county citizenry and retail investing, etc. The point is more options to the individual taxpayer to build their security and community, which begins to lower taxes for everyone. From my perspective, the stock market will have to increase returns, with guarantees, above the top-tier incentive rate in public-controlled capitalism for Texans to, even, consider releasing private savings to investment firms. It will be hard to convince Texans to do anything other than invest in their communities because of the tangible results; i.e., seeing your money transform peoples' lives in our communities can be very profound; the reimbursement of expenditures plus 5 or 8 percent, and the safety of no-loss principal (i.e., risk-free rate of 3 percent), will be hard to beat. We must instill a true commitment to all Texans the right way, not the cheap way.

CHAPTER 3

Community Restoration

> Trust is the foundation of leadership.
> —*21 Irrefutable Laws of Leadership* (sixth law)

Charles de Gaulle once said, "History does not teach fatalism…people get what they deserve." In other words, prepared leaders stand ready to meet the future; they do not react and are not surprised by anything, so this gives them power when it is time to move.

At this time in the year 2021 and beyond, our state leaders practice fatalism by treating critical moments: COVID-19, increasing poverty levels, highest uninsured population in the nation, forty-third in educational attainment while coming in thirty-ninth overall in education spending, and a downward spiraling economy that affects Texans' lives as inevitable, so they react to soften the misery, somewhat, and continue to depend on the federal government to help ease their responsibilities to the communities across Texas. What about being proactive leaders instead of corporate leaders? What about the foresight of equipping communities to become proud taxpaying citizens who know and can trust that their money is working for everyone?

Preparation is the key, and we all have a part. My imagination has led to a vision that is inescapable. For me, the burden must be laid bare to have relief. I fully realize that the person with the plan is the person with power, and I am prepared for the criticism from all angles, but the question is, are they prepared for me? Weariness has established itself within state programs, tax cuts, tax exemptions, propaganda reports, and state giveaways, for some time now, in my opinion.

It is time to give the communities of Texas, not counties, their long-awaited opportunity to do what GOD has intended all along— neighbor helping neighbor. Our governor, lieutenant governor, and the state legislature will be prepared to tell every Texan that "there is no money for such a gamble, the risk is too great!" In my mind, it is as good a time as any to give Texans the chance to show the tax collectors, what we are made of, and what we care about. I will give the state credit for cultivating an atmosphere of "learned helplessness," specifically in poor areas in every county across the state.

My position is that we do not know the awesome potential of what we leave behind in our "little country towns," hoping country folks make their way to the "big cities." Some Texans do not want to give up their quaint environments but would like to contribute at home in their community. This dilemma becomes clearer by the day; it is almost like Charles Dickens' *Tale of Two Cities*, but our problem is rural versus urban. There is no reason why we cannot have the best of both rural and urban living by using individual taxpayers in their communities, within their domiciled county, to give both advantaged and disadvantaged citizens real access to strong academic foundations in public schools and skilled vocational training that can lead innumerable directions. Some people will probably say, "This might limit people who should go to a four-year college." No, in fact, this helps whoever acquires vocational training by taming a chaotic mind with thinking processes, and it is impossible to predict the flow of ideas that may be derived. First, it gives people a way to make a good income while receiving a four- to five-year college education. Second, citizens can pay for higher education without student loans by taking methodical steps. And third, the person actually contributes to their community by allowing an individual taxpayer to pay for their skilled vocational trade to build their savings up.

See clearly, it is incumbent that state leaders promote community by making it customary in our counties (i.e., Texans' duty) to get a skilled vocational education through a community college paid by an individual taxpayer who will receive an incentive rate for guidance and the necessary support tools to ensure lifelong success, whether going to a four-year college or not. It is important that the "back-bone" of communities across this great land (i.e., individual taxpayers) be rewarded respectfully.

Every community in Texas wants to be strong, vibrant, and contribute to the place we all love, but it is made difficult by tradition, customs, folklore, and myths to keep the poor, poor and the middle class constrained through a system of elaborate federal and state mechanisms, which acquiesce to the "animal spirits" of the business world to give us unaffordable postsecondary education, inflationary pressures, unaffordable health insurance, and poor return rates on personal savings and retirement plans. Are you sure I am the inexperienced one, as you keep reading?

Do not look at my vision and plan for Texas from a money standpoint because the money is there to do whatever is necessary to reward individual taxpaying citizens, investing in their communities' future. Ask yourself this question, Do I want to keep paying ever-higher property and school taxes, or do I want to ensure the strategic expansion of the county tax base and get paid initial principal plus an incentive rate for investing in resident citizens to obtain the latest skilled vocational trades or strong academic foundations in our public schools to be what we want them to be, true taxpayers? The old adage "I cannot be what I alt to be because you cannot be what you alt to be" rings true not only in Texas but the world. If Texans want to end the divisiveness, bring us together; if Texans want to solve our environmental problems, bring us together in our communities where it all should begin.

In my big deal legislation, Texas communities are my main focus, and individual taxpayers are the beneficiaries; there will be no race, creed, color, or religion involved in the county skills fund or academic skills fund. In every independent school district, there will be two socioeconomic rungs—advantaged and disadvantaged—designating respectable returns for both, but the higher incentive rate will go to the disadvantaged (i.e., 8 percent), while the slightly lower incentive rate will go to the advantaged (i.e., 5 percent). And both rungs will be backed by a risk-free rate of 3 percent, this means failure is unacceptable, so, Texans, figure out what is lacking and supply it.

Every resident citizen who owns a home or land will have the automatic right reserved to invest their money in our most precious community capital—advantaged and disadvantaged citizens. And for county citizenry who choose not to own a home or land (called the buy-in citizens), they can purchase the right to invest in advantaged and disadvantaged citizens by paying the median property and school taxes in the county domiciled, every year by the deadline on January 31. Foresight into the big deal, suggest reinvigoration of individual taxpayers with a new sense of pride for their community, county, and Texas; the new atmosphere creates 100 percent, plus, tax compliance in every county, which leads, intuitively, to a real decline in taxes for the individual taxpayer, in the years ahead.

Homeowners, landowners, and buy-in citizens have only one restriction in community repair (three resident citizens at a time) to ensure quality and the necessary support, such as tuition, books, fees, licensure, and certification examination fees, mentoring, etc. for skilled vocational trade programs, that can include a built-in associate degree at the community college level. No true taxpayer is precluded from partnerships, meaning deals can be made in order to add more county citizens to the investment portfolio, a maximum of six investees, but will remain under the homeowner or landowner's name whom the agreement is made to keep equity in their community and a share of the incentive rate. Remember, the county skills fund and academic skills fund are for individual taxpayers to repair their communities and to reward "our" canons for investing at home, this is not for corporations. Individuals who work for corporations can invest in communities within their domiciled county because they are part of the community, paying property and school taxes.

The Community Protection Commission will be located in every county and appointed by the commissioners' court for three-year terms. The CPC will be paid positions, a body of five, and will reflect the demographic of the county; CPC will decide upon the depletion rate funding for the county skills fund, pay incentive rates, verify, validate, and track all investments in community college skilled vocational programs and built-in associate degrees, partnerships, and tax compliance. It will be necessary to have cooperation with the county treasurer, county clerk, and independent school district tax office, from time to time, which will be responsible for the academic skills fund and may work with the CPC. Texas Department of Criminal Justice-Huntsville, and community colleges across the state will work closely with the county tax office, county treasurer, county clerk, and state comptroller of Texas to deal effectively with the skills fund in every county, to invest in prisoners' skilled vocational training.

Texans, do not be afraid of my imagination, vision, and plan reflected in my message for your community; it is deservedly time for all the anguish and heartache the present has offered to give way to something unimaginable and supposedly impossible, until now. Our power lies in letting each Texan do what is natural—love, family, friends, community, and most importantly know that the future is what we make it for Texans. As a servant of GOD, our goal is not only to bear fruit but to help others do the same; we must be more than faithful, we must be fruitful (John 15:16).

Nothing else matters to me until the communities of Texas receive what is owed to them—affordable education for real incomes, affordable health care to take care of family, and respectable returns on hard-earned savings. The most complicated notion is helping people recognize to be successful as a state in having clean air, water, and a responsible society, will always be tied to what happens in your community; unfortunately, there will always be a new "stratagem theory" for more taxes by state and county bureaucracy to cover their inadequacies in dealing with the surrounding circumstances if we do not correct the problems, ourselves. How can our leaders talk about how magnificent Texas is when they obviously cannot stand to deal with or understand Texans? State leaders have an illogical and bizarre indifference toward our lives and the communities we choose to live. I know this because we feel it in our pocketbooks, see it in certain communities, and brush up against the deficiencies every day.

The sweeping big deal legislation and statewide referendum will pursue 30 percent of the Economic Stabilization Fund and select bureaucracy budgets, to go toward the skills fund in all 254 counties to encourage homeowners, landowners, and buy-in citizens to invest in county citizenry for skilled vocational trades, which, in turn, will begin to give individual taxpayers a sense of worth and a feeling of accomplishment through their contribution in helping others become fruitful in their community, and county. Do not let anyone distract with the politics of race because every time something gets close to resembling, what the Workers' Alliance Platform was all about, they interject covert messaging, "How you are different from me?" to divide when everyone has the same pressures of life—light bills, water bills, mortgages, car notes, health insurance, etc. They somehow create an "extraordinaire" type of nimbus with the explanations given, which lead nowhere except an unclear pathway to make a living for yourself and your family. In truth, I have no problem with the elites receiving state contracts, but what I cannot tolerate is depraving ordinary hardworking and retired citizens of their opportunity to receive an incentive rate (i.e., 8, 5, or 3 percent risk-free rate) for utilizing their own money in the most legitimate investment the world has ever known in my opinion—education.

There is no doubt in my mind that when the big deal legislation has the power to establish a skills fund in every Texas county, we will begin to have exponential innovation, which will yield unimaginable discernment abilities, therefore new industries. People are yearning to contribute in a way that matters, so I will give citizens direction and purpose. Just imagine, a "true" taxpayer in your community knocks on your door and asks, "Do you want to go to a diesel mechanic trade school?" You agree, and the individual taxpayer takes you to the local community college and enrolls you into the diesel mechanic trade school, but what you don't know is the trade school has integrated an atmospheric chemistry curriculum into the program to begin figuring out ways to eradicate or severely reduce carbon dioxide (i.e., exhaustive gases). The instructor stands in front of a gutted diesel engine discussing what happens as soon as the diesel fuel enters the engine and how the carbon dioxide is created through the mixtures of heat via the pistons, fuel injectors, engine block, etc. and exits by way of the exhaust system, emitting carbon dioxide into the atmosphere, troposphere to be exact. And then he or she begins to talk about the horrible effects carbon dioxide has on our environment, then the instructor states, "We must begin to figure out how to eliminate carbon dioxide as we work on building and fixing diesel engines." The students begin to put heavy thought into the problem as they work their way through school, working on diesel engines and discussing matters with fellow classmates. No one knows how these scenarios will end in our quest to end carbon dioxide emissions through "thinking, not tinkering" and the involvement of individual taxpaying citizens who care just as much as scientists. Keep in mind, there will be hundreds of thousands of thought-provoking applicable exercises that will be the foundation of vital industry in Texas, such as cement, air-conditioning, welding, heavy equipment, chemicals, aviation, oil and gas, etc. that will be repeated over and over across Texas in community colleges, committed to our intellectual might, community, and practical environmental cleaning technologies through individual taxpayer investors.

The scenario given above will unfurl throughout community colleges across Texas, creating a newfound excitement for cutting-edge technologies and trade skills backed by the skills fund in every county, dedicated to providing individual taxpayers with respectable returns (i.e., incentive rates), steering investment dollars toward social good. And accompanying strong emotions of social trust tied to societal needs, such as skilled education, mentoring, and authentic friendships, will give Texas advantages unforeseen. It is indescribable to quantitate, in words, the feeling of security when a person of meager means have someone (i.e., individual taxpayer) to give him or her the opportunity to obtain personal success as they contribute to collective prosperity in their community. This is the only way to sufficiently address our needs, compensating the individual taxpayer and improving lives of others through skilled education initially. Both will have a common purpose and direction, which will aid Texas in delivering for the United States and the world—clean air, land, and water, technologies.

Every action that I take, directly or indirectly, is meant to rejuvenate the most important part of all Texans' lives—family and community, no matter the socioeconomics. I am tired of people having to spend all their money on Wall Street to have a modicum of success with investments or other ventures when the investments desired the most are "next door." It is profound to witness the transformation of lives that you helped at home in your community instead of some piece of paper showing "performance growth" on an investment summary report. The tax collectors make it so complicated and convoluted that we forget that life happens where we live; we are to build solid ties throughout the county we call home. So, to create a tax base that ensures the longevity of family, friends, community, county, and state, this is the right order. There is no prosperity without ordinary Texans, therefore, the environment needed, most, must be brought into existence.

All I can do is lay bare, "What you see is what you get," as I run for the Forward Party-Texas Gubernatorial nomination in 2026, setting out a clear vision and justified plan for our great state that includes all Texans. Hope is not what I put in the state of Texas; I put it in the communities across Texas that form our big state. Most of our state leaders have a vested interest in keeping us divided on issues, which do not improve the lives of Texans like primary, secondary, postsecondary education (i.e., skilled vocational trades and traditional four-year college); affordable health care that everyone can afford to pay; and respectable returns on savings with longevity investments in the community. These are the "noble things" that require thinking skills, not perfunctory pontification, or tinkering skills. I seek to put everyone in a position to use their imagination about a state of being that utilizes all people, cultivates all talent, and enlists creative ways to solve all problems through our communities.

Do not think, for one minute, this vision and plan I have for our beloved Texas cannot happen. Texans are slowly but surely getting tired of living in "dismal infinity" described earlier in Chapter 1, p.21; there is no way toward life security for the common man or woman. Something is really wrong when our hardworking and retired citizens are put in compromised positions every day that questions your place in Texas, such as unaffordable and unattainable relevant skilled trades, skyrocketing health-care premiums with outlandish deductibles, and no reasonable way to obtain respectable and tangible returns on local savings accounts. To eliminate these insecurities, communities in Texas must have a surefire pathway toward achieving assurances at home in their community.

I believe in capitalism because it is the only economic system that can truly alter behavior and transform perceptions in what I am attempting to accomplish—maximize the GOD-given talent each of us possess. The efficacious remedy is a county skills fund and an academic skills fund in each of the 254 counties in Texas that encourages individual taxpayers to take an interest in developing minds for the sake of their community, county, and state. "Mount Impossible" will be climbed but in a strategic, methodical manner that gives deference to citizens who pay property and school taxes in their domiciled county and buy-in citizens, who will pay the median tax of both—property and school, all for the right to be a part of building community enlightenment neighborhood by neighborhood. See clearly, if all Texans must pay their way in our state, then we must prepare them to do so through capable, willing citizens, and they must receive an incentive rate to do this all-important work.

Community restoration, in my opinion, gives back and returns what is rightfully your responsibility, as a citizen, to improve or to make anew. In order for this to occur, a prevailing set of conditions must be everlasting to ensure strong investment in both advantaged and disadvantaged citizens. The incentive rate plus reimbursements are necessary tools for success. And the most critical component, the risk-free rate (i.e., 3 percent) creates the necessary "safety zone" individual taxpayers need to be fully committed to community restoration, (review illustration on page 25).

One way or another, I need dollars flowing back to communities to be creatively placed in the hands of individual taxpaying citizens who pay property and school taxes. It has to promote social improvements in a serious way, putting money to work like $20 to $50 billion in education over a four-year period. The majority of the money, if not all, will go to individual taxpayers from the county skills fund and academic skills fund—operated by independent school districts. I want to make certain that everyone is accessible, whether rich or poor. All Texans must be prepared to pay their share of taxes, so the only wise thing to do is give communities their incorruptible inheritance (i.e., the right to improve the lives of others) all the way from primary education to community college.

There are some things that happen in our lives we all regret and can never take back, but if we are willing to push past the toil and circumstance, new views emerge—becoming a better person because of it. Now apply the same reasoning to governing; our state government is supposed to learn from their mistakes and never to make the same egregious mistakes again and again, yet they continue to compound problems with the rote routines of irrelevant job training and state benefits with harsh penalties. All of which lead nowhere but frustration to both recipients and individual taxpayers. Unfortunately, our state leaders and bureaucracy will not yield to community prosperity, so we must get rid of all the elected and nonelected officials, Democrats or Republicans, who stand in the way of community restoration. Do not feel sorry for them; they deserve all the criticism, that goes along with fatalism, that can be heaped upon their heads. How have we become so disenfranchised and disenchanted in Texas? The answer, we replaced Texans' right to have an interest in their community citizenry with state agency, student loans, and stocks & bonds, by getting away from the human element. Understand, I am not against state agencies, student loans, and Wall Street—they have their place—but these "bureaucratic" regressions, not progressions, will always remain irrelevant in building real Texans; it is the community's purpose. The bridge to the twenty-first century is within all of us, therefore it will always flow through communities if I am blessed to be the servant leader of our state, i.e., the new governor of Texas.

Communities must be protected yet coexist with capitalism as individual taxpaying citizens equip citizenry to live within it. There is no socialist agenda here, just a creative vision with a plan to implement a new future for Texans using 30% of public money wisely and efficiently, which makes certain that our lives are marked with perseverance and resilience. We have settled for way too little in the "conversations of our time" community, education, health care, and return rates on savings. Again, do not be afraid of my direction; it is time for all Texans to come together and settle this abomination of fruitlessness. Everybody knows our purpose is empty; it is instinctively heartfelt, without all, we continue to stumble around in the dark when all is needed is a candle.

In Matthew 7:24–27, the scripture instructs us to "build the house on a rock, and rain descends, the flood came, and the winds blew and beat the house, and it did not fall." This is the only foundation that makes sense for both advantaged and disadvantaged citizens in Texas. Why would Texas foolishly build its house on the sand in the twenty-first century? Or will we be like a foolish man who built his house on sand, and the rain descended, the flood came, and the winds blew and beat that house—and it fell, and great was its fall? Every day, our state leaders fail to focus on restoring our communities across Texas. We quicken instability and beyond; this is why capitalism needs a community-based competitor, with "vested interest" that operates above everything else, always rewarding and repairing communities, keeping us all full of hope for tomorrow.

Hope is meant to be strange; it can appear out of nowhere yet always there. Anticipation, expectation, and optimism all drive the strongest emotion in the universe, which ultimately leads to fulfillment. Therefore, I strive to place a vision and plan before Texans to not only feel but imagine. We all see the wrong done in our state governance, and it must be rectified in a sane-orderly way that recognizes contributing members of society and simultaneously encourage county citizenry to seek economic and social justice, no matter the category for all. Texans need to see good actions, good character, and good people in their immediate vicinity (i.e., community) to get the desired effect of the strongest emotion in the universe—hope. We can win against any economic injustice, environmental problem, or social ailment in our communities.

Note: It would clearly be disingenuous of me to write about my vision and plan for communities across Texas and not mention the serious problem I have with the office of the Texas comptroller.

This office pressures county appraisal districts to increase property values and by default increase school taxes, continuing the drain on homeowner and landowner finances, who get nothing in return for dedicated cooperation. Within the statewide referendum, I will call on the powers of the Texas governor, asking the citizens of the state to allow the appointment of two offices: state's attorney general and comptroller. There has to be adherence in giving citizens of Texas "breathing room." so to invest in the future of their communities, there must be serious consequences for county appraisal districts who do not conform. Modest increases, 1% to 2%, every three to five years is what I favor, because the investment in communities to obtain "cutting-edge" technical or vocational skills and beyond will expand the tax base over time. Government is here forever, albeit, federal, state, or county, so encourage and give hope to the communities that will make our counties and state mighty. There will not be community restoration if citizens do not have the capacity to improve their lives (i.e., real incomes) and maintain their responsibilities: education, health-care insurance, and retirement savings, without knowledge and wisdom from experienced individuals within our communities.

CHAPTER 4

Public School Finance: Robin Hood

Anyone can steer a ship, but it takes a leader to chart the course.
—*21 Irrefutable Laws of Leadership* (fourth law)

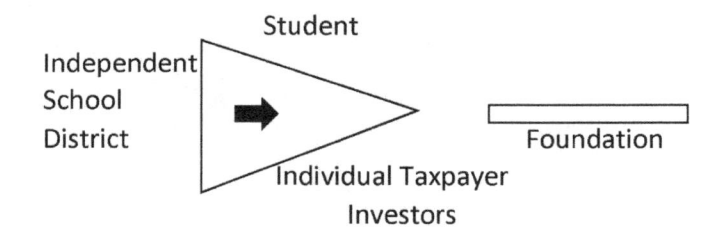

Model explanation. There is a deliberate wall placed between the independent school district and the funds they will provide for the academic skills fund, to allow individual taxpayers to do their investing—work with primary and secondary students. The arrow pointing in a forward direction signifies everyone's mission—a strong academic foundation for each student. I envision independent school districts throughout the state funding academic skill funds for the sake of their commitment to community and institution. The recipients of the fund's incentive rates will be individual taxpayer investors, who pay property and school taxes in their domiciled county. An individual investor may choose up to three students to help, i.e., to aid in building an all-important academic foundation. The community investor will need the necessary permission from parents to work with students after school, on weekends, or during traditional summer break. The full academic skills fund illustration for individual taxpayer investors will be at the end of chapter 4.

Keep this simplistic synergistic model in mind as one of two core investment tools for homeowners, landowners, and buy-in citizens to ensure foundational success in primary-secondary academia and to increase individual taxpayers' savings, (i.e., disposable or retirement funds), in every Texas county.

First and foremost, I am not advocating for any change as to how independent school districts educate within their system. This is about what happens after school, on weekends, and during traditional summer break, creating investment opportunities in young lives that are key to our future economic and financial prosperity. It is time to create an equity stake in our youth that reflects their importance to their communities, county, and state. It is critical to understand the all-out total commitment that will be placed in education (i.e., vocational skills with certifications, licensures, and associate degrees), but to get to this juncture, the independent school districts must do their part. Note, my plan places education and community above everything else.

I have no interest in what independent school district administrators might say, "We cannot do this," or "We cannot afford to do this." Remember, ISD-administrators are just like our state leaders— take from Texans and give nothing in return. These institutions are a critical building block in our communities and county tax base; citizens are proud of their schools despite the insensitivity to their kitchen table issues, formerly mentioned, but now I seek to have them "give back" by creating an investment tool (i.e., academic skills fund) that will place emphasis on rewarding the community for aiding in shaping young minds. Look at it like this—the academic skills fund is inversely related to the penalties in interest that the authorities assess in late fees for property and school taxes; meaning the "fund" does not scare Texans into paying their obligation but ensure cooperation through financial incentives, which will strengthen the bonds of community with involvement.

This is not just about the future of young people, but it is also about the future of responsible adults who deposit their hard-earned money in banks and get literally "0 percent interest," therefore, no real incentive to save. On the surface, you would be right to think, *Wait a minute, this is a federal issue*, but the federal government has nothing to do with how we choose to reward and repair our states' communities. If elected governor of Texas, my direction creates investment tools for communities that give our citizens a reason to save money and be rewarded for it. The reward is given in the form of incentive rates that focus on primary-secondary education, and post-secondary skilled vocational trades, which is separate from the independent school district's academic skills fund but can work together with the counties' skills fund as a "feeder."

Independent school districts and community colleges are the investments of choice because they embody the very essence of social good. Our state and national leaders have always neglected involving the individual taxpayer, who always seems to miss the benefit of the "individual" along with collective prosperity at the community level. It will always remain an imperative that our individual taxpayers have an efficient means of investment in "life infrastructure" (i.e., education, health care, and retirement savings) for themselves and an incentive to do it for others. We must get out of the, somehow, indoctrinated notion of benevolence when every life hangs in the balance with pocketbook issues that will always center around real incomes—life improvement issues, affordable health care, and disposable and retirement savings. How do independent school districts finance "top-notch" football stadiums and other buildings and not be forced to create an academic skills fund for individual taxpayers to recuperate their tax dollars and promote social good through educating the young? The answer is clear, they do not care about anything other than the institution that sustains, both, themselves, i.e., selfishness, and their stature in certain communities, but it should be all communities.

What I fear most for communities is to be afraid of something new that will always remain unimaginable to some, but somehow, being convinced, the "old system" should be feared less, when you already see the proof. Listen, any social good distributed by bureau-cracy (i.e., school districts and state government programs that severely discount the value of community and place a strong empha-sis, future value, on state agency or proxies and use our money) cannot and will not be successful in whatever they foresee for "the greater good" because there is no constructive means to involve the individual taxpayer, canons, who bears the larger burden in what is trying to be accomplished; therefore, these state or school programs are reduced to activities instead of accomplishments. Take note, my constructive criticism is all about making Texas a better place to be rich, middle-class, marginalized, an immigrant, or a child to prepare Texans to take care of themselves. I am the only one with the imagi-nation, vision, and plan to merge social good (i.e., primary, second-ary, postsecondary education—skilled vocational trades) into "home-grown" financial instruments that create the effect—"force majeure", which encourages "fervent spirits" to do good works through guided experiences and community coherence to make all Texans better in the end, then the beginning.

Texans will get the form of respect deserved at home from Jack Daniel Foster Jr. Your castle and domain must include the indepen-dent school district(s) that lie within your domiciled county to erad-icate learned helplessness, poverty, close-mindedness, and whatever the troubles outside school. It has always been unsettling to me that independent school districts "wash their hands" of students after their senior year. Every student, no matter where in Texas, should be prepared to handle the rigors of life not only in school but outside it as well; therefore, independent school districts in Texas must bear responsibility to communities they serve with helping facilitate the outgrowth of future property and school taxpayers by funding the academic skills fund for individual taxpayers to benefit economically and financially in their county. On the surface, it is a praiseworthy gift to be appreciated, but the money extends far beyond the sur-face into a realm of commitment to each community, which estab-lishes equity in our education system by compelling citizens to right wrongs and do more for those who have been mistreated. No federal, state, or county bureaucrat can compete with the amount of influence, pressure, and reach Texans will have in their communities via a charted course, set forth.

It might be subtle, but young people will get to experience, up close, the preamble to the constitution of the United States: establishment of justice, ensuring domestic tranquility, and the promotion of the general welfare. But these three virtues cannot be deeply embedded in one's being without individual taxpaying citizens having a conducive environment to invest their dollars in county citizenry, pursuant to the fourth virtue: "Secure the Blessings of Liberty to ourselves and our Posterity."

The fourth virtue is the most prolific source of ingenuity that will take independent school districts and the state of Texas into the twenty-first century; these uncharted waters will not only give focus to the fundamentals in education (i.e., reading, writing, and arithmetic) but provide much-needed attention to preparing young people to be good stewards of their communities—taxpayers and caretakers of the environment (i.e., land, water, and air). There can be no holding back; we must go all-out if Texas schools are to be successful for students and community, befitting both. Our lives literally depend on having a heightened sense of inclusion—"the quintet" to be involved in the lives of others, seeing our citizenry through to success and also rewarding homeowners, landowners, and buy-in citizens for the most important job in Texas—repairing our communities.

The pathway to the heart is showing a deep understanding of what matters most in Texans' lives: family, close friends, and community. To allow for a more communal approach, which gives a real sense of belonging, our independent school districts' academic skills fund combined with the counties' skills fund will be the empowerment and hope needed throughout our great land for our homeowners, landowners, and buy-in citizens to be rewarded as they take on the job that is only meant for townsman, not federal, state, or county government. My vision and plan coalesce significantly serious opportunities and grave responsibility, with economic-financial interest, for homeowners, landowners, and buy-in citizens to not only receive, but give in the form of both community contributions and solutions, to the most widespread problem in the world—poverty.

It should be no secret that I am about "us" and "we," not "them" or "they." As a thinking man, I realize it is the institution of community that will make or break the next thirty-five to fifty years for Texans, so it is paramount, noble, and a noteworthy direction to set forth for the unforeseen in a manner that creates the everlasting power of inclusion,—giving everyone the capacity to reject their "lot in life" to contribute and benefit upon becoming an individual taxpayer who pays property and school taxes to promote well-being and education. We already know, investment in education generates income for the individuals who obtain it, but what about the added dimension of life guidance in the formable years coupled with education? It should be commonplace that Texans can derive investment income from—working with students—in their independent school district(s), adding to their portfolios or savings accounts. I aim to put school districts in a position to not only adequately fund their schools with solid financial forecasting and concrete funding but pay respectable classroom teacher salaries. And help with funding the academic skills fund in every school district by redirecting both sin (100%) and lottery (30%) tax revenue in a direction that will impact lives and bank accounts in communities.

Answer this question: if you judge a fish based on its ability to climb a tree, what would the fish think? Albert Einstein answered, "The fish would think it is stupid," and I agree. I cannot be held to a standard that is not becoming of my ability and inconsequential to our lives. I do not think like traditional politicians, they like to "tinker," and I am a thinker, so the comparison would be difficult. They like state bureaucracy, I do not. I am about figuring out ways to repair and reward communities with a purpose; traditional politicians will agree but have no real idea how to start or maybe literally "think" it is silly. *The Message: A Time for Repair and Reward in Texas Communities* is a critical read to understanding me, but also a standard by which to hold outmoded political tinkering. We need ideas that are doable and realistic with real impact, outside state-bureaucratic reach. This is not throwing money at a problem, but this is methodically thinking it through, creating a community investment mindset, replacing old traditions and haphazard thoughts that do nothing for preparing Texans to be motivated to lead in all categories of industry and education. I do not want Texans to think my plan for community transformation is unrealistic, it is the right course of action. Always remember that our state constitution is a malleable document that is capable of being altered with a statewide referendum, or the state legislature can act themselves. I am not incline to wait on legislative action, so my preference is the statewide referendum, to show legislators this is not a caste system.

We must remake a small portion of public capital that will be focused on community, front and center, to extend beyond our economic system, biased toward hard work, savings, skilled vocational trades, and building solid educational foundations; this begins with independent school districts in Texas correcting course and literally paying homage to individual citizens who pay property and school taxes or the median of both by inviting them to work with the educational institution as a stakeholder, investing in young peoples' future. Understand that this small portion of directed capital will not only be a money multiplier for individual taxpayers but will also be a multiplier of hope and preparedness for the unforeseen. I aim to convince Texans that we must have a society that respects communities and their right to use constructive and creative endeavors to improve the lives of local citizenry through the use of institutions redesigned to "share" along with the full commitment of Texas. The alternative is to allow capitalism to continue the predictable pattern of extracting more and more capital out of communities, which cycles right back to Wall Street, when working capital can best serve the place you call home, by producing tangible results.

Capitalism left to its own vices seems to think the market itself will suffice; it could not be further from the truth as unchecked independent school districts routinely pick football stadiums and bare-bones budgeting in "classrooms" over the general welfare and "Knowledge building and sharing" with communities, students, and teachers. Do not take my strong critique of our school districts' multiple failures to establish nobility in society or the concern for our economic system, capitalism, as a projected dislike for either. This is the problem, capitalism by nature will always seek high prices for profit; therefore, our state leaders cannot get a handle on the "hidden matter" that constantly haunts not only Texas but the nation. Since there is no real "taming" capitalism, Texans must be given the ability to outsmart the system in key areas essential to life and success (i.e., education, health care, and increase returns on disposable or retirement savings) so, we must make capitalism conform to us as we continue to work within it, we will enter the extremity of its borders, not the inner workings of it. Knowing how to compete and insulate from capitalism locally through the utilization of homeowners, landowners, and buy-in citizens with protected incentive rates to do the "good work" of investing in community for the enhancement of the quintet (i.e., rich, middle-class, marginalized, children, and immigrants) will begin to induce a second enlightenment within capitalism—epoch.

Primary and secondary schools will be a vital component of investment for individual taxpayers because independent school districts' academic skills fund will not wavier from the incentive rate established no matter capitalism's reaction to our local economies. We have to signal what is important to Texans in the twenty-first century; money and economy are important, but the notion of winners and losers in our communities make no sense. Citizens who lack the proper guidance early in their lives struggle to find their way, so it is left up to the community to be "hands-on" in modeling and molding a responsible citizenry. Community is the key component in eliminating "winners and losers"—socioeconomic characterization, so we must perpetually prepare citizens to do their part in our state, bottom-up, not top-down.

Our fellow American citizens outside the state will be anxiously watching as the bold moves proceed to rightfully reclaim what belongs to community—properly maximizing citizenry potential through individual taxpayers. Intuitively, I know this is right because no state or federal agency has the power through a "wasteful government program." It belongs to Texans in communities to do.

The mark of GOD's people is a community that extends its hand to all socioeconomic groups with lasting enthusiasms because the mystery is not knowing who will be the one or ones with the simple solutions to the most complex problems of the day in Texas and the nation. So it will not be wise to curb our "public capacity" in any form. It has become too easy to "dismiss" bona fide ideas that are worthy of exploration, so we must go inward to regenerate Texas. The excitement is hard to contain for me because I can foresee communities finally coming to terms with "human progress" that can naturally fit us all in, so to establish justice, ensure domestic tranquility, promote the general welfare, and most importantly, "secure the Blessings of Liberty to ourselves and Our Posterity"—your family.

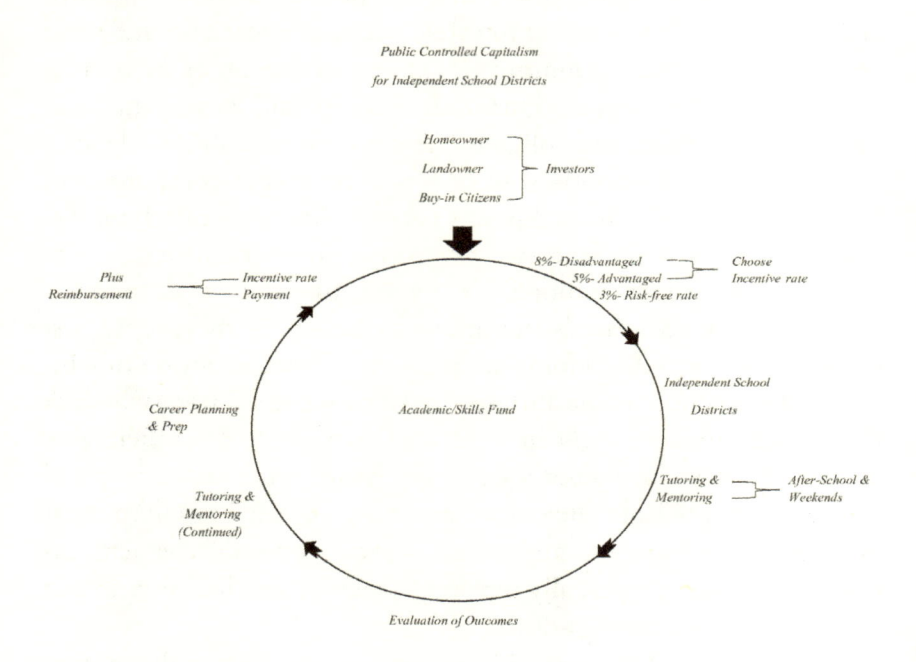

Explanation to follow.

Public-Controlled Capitalism: Academic Skills Fund

Public-controlled capitalism-academic skills fund follows the same concept as the skills fund in counties, except it is less intense but offers additional investment to individual taxpayers; this is more of a focus on tutoring and developing the mind with introductions to the vast skilled vocational trades relevant to our future before possibly pursuing a traditional four-year degree.

First, I am not advocating for any change to our independent school districts within the system; this is about creating ways for individual taxpayers to have investment opportunities, involvement in building strong community ties, which fits Texas' blossoming and budding future. Imagine the possibilities for intellectual growth if a young student is caught in the early stages of trouble or a learning disability and set on the right path by an individual taxpayer investor, who is genuinely concerned about correcting the problem. The big deal will mandate all school districts in Texas to use their money with efficacy by adding the concept of public-controlled capitalism, creating an academic skills fund to allow individual taxpayers to regain relevance in their communities and obtain incentive rates for time and effort spent with students chosen to mentor. Both advantaged and disadvantaged students will have access to new learning, new experiences, and different environments after school and on weekends (i.e., outside the education system in their county).

There is an infinite capacity for year-round investment, whether the school is nine or twelve months, as long as homeowners, landowners, and buy-in citizens are involved. When superintendents come before the voting public asking for more money, local taxpayers will capitulate if money is shared in a productive manner. Sacred institutions will need to "step outside the box" and have more concern for debtors, not just themselves.

Homeowners, landowners, and buy-in citizens

At the very top of the illustration, there are three distinct investors: homeowners, landowners, and buy-in citizens. Homeowners and landowners have automatic privileges for investment in local students because they pay property and school taxes, yearly. Buy-in citizens, non-owners or renters, can pay the median tax rate, property and school, in their domiciled county to reserve the right to invest in school-age citizenry. All taxes must be paid by January 31.

Incentive rates

The homeowner, landowner, and buy-in citizen can pursue advantaged or disadvantaged students for any necessary help to support their education, only three at a time, for tutoring, life lessons, etc., but receiving the highest incentive rate of 8 percent will be reserved for the most vulnerable in communities because it is extremely important that all students have equal access to the necessary support structures, tools of learning. Investment in students will include the principal (i.e., expenditures on books, school supplies, educational trips, food, Wi-Fi connections) along with tutoring and mentoring—anything educational. Upon successful completion, or not, reimbursement of monetary value will be awarded along with incentive rate, but the in-kind benefits far exceed money.

Risk-free rate

The risk-free rate is for either advantaged or disadvantaged students (i.e., investee for successful completion of grade level or not). If failure should occur for whatever reason, the investor can cash out and receive payment of expenditures plus 3 percent. We are sending two signals, just like in the adult version of public-controlled capitalism: do not give up on your community, and every Texan is a valued citizen, advantaged or disadvantaged. There is absolutely no reason why every student, unless a learning disability is consistently documented, in our state cannot be prepared to become a true tax-paying, law-abiding citizen, courtesy of homeowners, landowners, and buy-in citizens within their county.

The tax office of every school district will be responsible for validations and documentation of all educational endeavors taxpayers pursue for students; they will also be responsible for payment of reimbursements and incentive rates to the investor. Incentive pay and reimbursement will be distributed after a year and a day, for tax purposes; the Community Protective Commission could be available for guidance and record sharing.

To participate with school-age students, primary or secondary, the taxpayer must be free of any criminal record.

Parents must give consent through documentation that an individual taxpayer can help their child.

Independent School Districts

I am referring to public independent school districts, not chartered, Montessori schools, or private schools. It is fair for individual taxpayers, who have children in these school types formerly listed, to invest in students attending area public schools, if they so choose. This approach will give all school districts ample funding power and the needed help outside the classroom to formulate good citizens. There should be a noticeable difference when individual taxpayers get involved with students after school, on weekends, and during traditional summer break to further reinforce educational learning and life experiences.

After school and weekends

To truly help a school-age student, primary or secondary, deficient in any area, an individual taxpayer investor will need to do tutoring after school or help pupils on the weekend. There is a third option, hire a teacher from the school district or a retired teacher. Remember that I have stated "reimbursement for anything educational" to work with a student one-on-one until success has been obtained and then move on to the next learning experience.

Mentoring in someone's life is essential, whether school-age or adult. I want every possible moment to count—ensure the student is not detached from an interesting world, give students confidence, be a model citizen for students, talk to them about responsible living (continuing education, health insurance, and retirement savings), answer their questions honestly, etc. Time and effort can really shape a young life for the better.

Evaluation of outcomes

Probably the most important aspect of the independent school districts'—academic skills fund will be the noticeable changes in students' attitudes about their new future, community support, and intellectual growth in and out of the classroom. And because parents allowed their child to be tutored and mentored by an individual taxpayer, they may be notified of their impact on students' academic successes or failures, and behavior.

Tutoring and mentoring continued

This is meant to be ongoing despite grade-level success and evaluation of outcomes. It will be up to the individual taxpayer to follow the same three students from elementary to high school graduation, or mentor and tutor someone new. Always be a resource that the student can count on, even if the outside educational experiences are completed.

Career planning

Every student needs to have a direction and actionable plan to accomplish goals set in life, so this will be a perfect inlet to help students understand the same, "well-versed", individual taxpayer can invest in their life for skilled vocational trades of all kinds (i.e., maximum three years in the same trade) before thinking about a four-year college. Again, mentoring can go a long way in having realistic outcomes for student success.

Plus reimbursement

The biggest feature of both the county skills fund and academic skills fund is granting the reimbursement of all money spent during the investment period along with the incentive rate or risk-free rate. It is the right thing to do because your tax dollars will build the society that we all want to live in, and besides the time and effort individual taxpayer investors will expend to build that society should be rewarded.

CHAPTER 5

Economic Stabilization Fund (Rainy Day Fund)

Leaders find a way for the team to win.
—*21 Irrefutable Laws of Leadership* (fifteenth law)

Most Texans, probably, have no idea about "our" economic stabilization fund because it is state government's "rabbit out of the hat" trick when money gets tight or some unnecessary project comes along, they want to pursue, which has nothing to do with repairing and rewarding communities. By the way, our fund is the largest of all states; we have $12 to $15 billion saved, maybe more. Approximately 85 percent of the money in the economic stabilization fund comes from oil and gas, so there will be no talk or disruption from me about eliminating our status as the number one oil producer and refiner in the United States. Do not be disheartened by my honest statement, in fact, be encouraged because this paves the way for what we will do for Texas communities and the environment (i.e., air, land, and water). A little clue, the Tenth Amendment to the United States Constitution—powers reserved to the states is a very powerful paragraph that will forever prevent the "Green New Deal" from entering Texas; this is why my plan will have serious implications for the other forty-nine states.

To have a real impact on the lives of Texans in their communities, I will seek a statewide referendum on the powers of the Texas governor. In order to effectively maneuver in any given situation without bothering the lieutenant governor and the state legislature, I will boldly ask Texans to grant the Texas governor yearly discretion over 30 percent of the economic stabilization fund coupled with the authority to extract 30 percent from all state agencies that have no consequential bearing on Texans' lives. And I will also be asking for the power to appoint the Texas attorney general and comptroller because these two offices could cripple my economic and financial agenda for Texas communities, and here is why: first, we will need the state comptroller to not increase property taxes for three to five years no matter the home improvement or booming economic activity in areas around the state; secondly, the attorney general must prosecute to the fullest extent of the law anyone who abuses the academic skills fund created and funded by independent school districts, with financial assistance from the sin tax (100%) and state lottery (30%), and the county skills fund within each county for community improvement; both "funds" will be the new symbols of social good, and social trust. The abuse has to do with classifications, advantaged or disadvantaged, the incentive rate will be higher if an individual taxpayer invest in a disadvantaged citizen (i.e., 8 percent) rather than an advantaged citizen, which will be 5 percent, so, these issues are for the Community Protection Commission and independent school districts to scrutinize closely, because both proxies will be held accountable.

The 30 percent of the economic stabilization fund will be used to establish and fund, every legislative year, the skills fund in every county along with legislation mandating contributions based on population in all 254 counties, think Dillon's rule. I anticipate approximately $11 to $15 million of tax-free money going to each counties' skills fund from the state for homeowners, landowners, and buy-in citizens, who pay property and school taxes, to be incentivized to invest in their communities for skilled vocational trades and other necessary tools for success. The contribution by rural counties with a population of less than a million will make a payment of $2 million every legislative year to the counties' skills fund, and urban counties with a population greater than one million people will pay $5 million per one million populous every legislative year. Reasonable depletion rates will establish county contributions over time to ensure the skills fund is well funded and allow citizens to receive respectable returns for taking care of their citizens and a risk-free rate of 3 percent for unforeseen problems. The skills fund within every county will be separate from all county government accounts and budgets; accounting work will be done by the county treasurer and county clerk. The Community Protection Commission, public face, will pay incentive rates plus principal to individual taxpaying citizens—cash, do the record keeping, and investigative work for validity purposes.

The economic stabilization fund represents a fresh start with renewed purpose in communities and Texas. The community is the only chance we have to get this right; the bickering in national and state politics must be drowned out, so, the real work can be done- preparing our citizens to become three-dimensional taxpayers (i.e., sales tax, property, and school) instead of one dimensional with government assistance. The time has come for "Infallible nuanced" thinking with a constant well-spring of wisdom to implement a plan that will super-bound every citizen to Texas' economic-financial interest. Think beyond capitalism into the realm of prosperity to ourselves and our posterity. It is a different sphere of thinking because it frees socioeconomic groups from the worries of not having the ability to contribute three-dimensionally by giving this responsibility with incentives to homeowners, landowners, and buy-in citizens to equip citizenry to be what we want them to be—law-abiding, productive citizens.

George Washington Carver wrote, "No individual has any right to come into this world and go out of it without leaving behind him or her a distinct and legitimate reason for having passed through it." This simple yet profound statement holistically defines the responsibilities of mankind, Texans, and what "social capital" is supposed to represent; it is to be redirected to allow the experienced among us to deliver the "distinct and legitimate" reasons we are on earth in the first place, tutelage. We will begin our earnest quest of delivering 30 percent of the economic stabilization fund, 30 percent of all inconsequential government bureaucracy monies, and county government contributions to the skills fund in three years or less, due to odd legislative years. I want Texans to know, there are people in our state government who will resist and hide behind traditional bureaucracy, any so-called statute of law they can find or just have fear of being irrelevant. Do not worry, I will point it out every step of the way, so this can never happen again—denying Texans the right and authority to care for others, with incentives.

No plan has any chance of success without homeowners, landowners, and buy-in citizens having a purpose within it and the ability to share in the creation of wealth through community efforts for ourselves and posterity. The only way to capture the great might of the quintet (i.e., rich, middle-class, marginalized, children, and immigrants) is to unharness it, with structured investment-my plan. The idea is to put forth both the academic skills fund for independent school districts and the counties' skills fund, so all can have a way to enrich their lives. It is important in life to display sufficient experience in responsibilities to no longer be under a tutor. GOD has truly blessed those who have had the necessary tutelage in their lives to be the citizens that Texas expects, but we must know that it is intended to be extended to the less fortunate as well. Think about it, imagine what 30 percent of the economic stabilization fund and 30 percent of insignificant state agencies' budgets redirected toward incentives, so communities can build toward affording life's infrastructure (i.e., education, health care, personal savings) and reinforcing sub-structure (individual investors), for all socioeconomic groups could mean? There is only one way to prepare Texans for our nation's way of life—capitalism, and that is structured homegrown-investment, which will allow individual taxpayers the honor "at-home" to repair and be rewarded for a job I know will be well-done, for community and county.

Our chance to secure ordinary lives in communities across Texas is now, by giving homeowners, landowners, and buy-in citizens their deserved right, divine right, to secure personal savings for retirement and recreation through investment in others to improve their lives. In turn, citizens in all socioeconomic groups will begin to have excitement and hope for the future because everyone is a tangible part of it. There should be no lack of options for citizens to constantly improve their lives, no excuses; individual taxpaying citizens will stand ready to afford fellow Texans the ability to take care of themselves and family.

No precedent exists in state government that lends itself to acting in-favor of our communities, so it would be well-founded to call for a statewide referendum to amend the constitution, seeking more power to the governor, which will move us toward the twenty-first century—community investment. As it stands now, if elected governor, the attempt to use 30 percent of the economic stabilization fund and strip select state bureaucracies of 30 percent, constitutionally, the lieutenant governor can stop what I seek for Texans. The actions I will take will give meaning to being governor of Texas because I do not look at this office as just a "seat or title," it is about impacting lives in ways that change destiny for both what can be seen and unseen. In my mind, I have to let people know I care about our lives. Unfortunately, invalid reasons exist as to why Texans cannot gain access to higher education through individual taxpayers, Texans cannot afford health insurance for their families, and Texans cannot obtain respectable returns on personal savings. The governorship is supposed to be about solutions, not dissolutions, to these specific kitchen table issues first and foremost. Without answers to community angst, we will persist in this tenuous state of uncertainty—brokenness.

My biblical hero, King Solomon, son of King David, reigned approximately forty years, and in that reign, all the peoples' needs were met. He was enabled by having an understanding heart toward his people. When our state leaders care more about "Texas-coffers" and "Texas-fame" instead of Texans, our lives will always remain in peril, vulnerable to Adam Smith's "animal spirits." I aim to make the citizens of Texas the priority again. Somehow we got off course, but in truth, we never were on the right course. We always need sustained and protected investment in communities, "exigent"—capitalism, that create awareness of the importance of life at home. The governor of Texas must be bigger than the "seat occupied," exceeding it in every way in thought and compassion for Texans and communities. Indeed, it is rare that we get an opportunity to capture a moment in time such as this where elected state and federal officials are actually "Too small" for the "big seats" that represent Texas. If we are to meet the needs of Texans, an understanding of what is relevant to community life should reign supreme. To have an understanding heart is to understand we all have core needs that must be met albeit advantaged or disadvantaged citizens. A leader must recognize the linchpin that tethers all Texans—taxes—and seek to reinforce this bond through individual taxpayers, at home, in our communities we all love.

My confidence in Texans far exceeds our elected state leaders. I see a way to rectify wrongs by using the economic stabilization fund and select state government agencies in a tax-free efficient manner. I will not concern myself with "governing losses" for three years due to the fact that our statehouse never bothered to concern themselves with ordinary citizens' pain at the kitchen table. Our state government owes Texas homeowners and landowners, so the best way to show my appreciation for being a dedicated taxpayer of property and school taxes is to freeze property values and create community investment instruments (i.e., county skills fund for adults and academic skills fund for primary and secondary education, both will pay incentive rates, plus principal). It is extremely important for people to see these actions because this reset county coffers, increasing tax revenue from buy-in citizens and the new highly skilled workers that enter local markets every year afterwards. The state can decrease or increase taxes at will; that is easy, but that does nothing to increase the tax base in order to lower taxes. I am about creating a three-dimensional taxpayer who will pay property, school, and sales taxes either as a homeowner, landowner, or buy-in citizen, willfully. When the attachment to Texas is strengthened, social trust develops, so the excitement about state budget shortfalls or the economic stabilization fund dwindling will be unfounded. Credibility far exceeds the capacity of money in every way, so wherever the deficit lies, I will tell Texans the situation, pay "our" debt and figure out another incentive strategy. The job of state governance is not to make money, it is about creating avenues for dollars to cycle back to "social good" therefore creating "social trust", not public good or public trust, too vague; I will use economic—financial means that benefit individual taxpayers in working with their community, not against it.

I choose my words carefully and place heavy emphasis on essential, imperative, and necessary in what I am about to say; it is essential to our state that the quintet affords the ability to improve their life situation or circumstance in order to become a three-dimensional taxpayer; it is an imperative in our state the quintet has the ability to afford health insurance, with no financial harm, at reasonable prices for themselves and family without dependence upon any state agency; it is also necessary for our state to afford the quintet the ability to obtain respectable returns on personal savings, despite our ongoing national interest rate struggles, for working and retired Texans. Governing is about prioritizing and choosing. I just come down on the side of ordinary people in communities across Texas instead of corporations. The economic stabilization fund together with "big deal" legislation will actually enhance "big business" position because when individuals are incentivized to help their community acquire technical skills, the workforce becomes strengthened in unlimited confidence and knowledge, making it easier for companies to hire and focus on their production processes and marginal profits, leaving the education of workers in the hands of the "shepherds" who live in these communities.

Let me elaborate on the 30 percent I want to extract from state agencies that do not impact our lives in a manner equal to the struggle at the kitchen table. What would happen when funds are cut 30 percent at the General Land Office? This is an office that sits on a billion dollars from a federal grant while poor and working-class people have to labor, i.e., paperwork, to get assistance, why? Does the Texas Commission on Environmental Quality affect your life in any impactful way? I honestly do not know the purpose of testing the air, land, and water with no enforcement of stiff fines, which should have crippling effects or collecting data that has no real application. What about these area councils throughout the state such as Galveston Area Council, do these proxies give real meaning to "state government-cowardice" or what? These councils make counties compete for grants of your local money, which cycle back to the state capitol. The unfortunate part about the whole thing is that every county prefers to renovate buildings or build new ones, leaving the county citizens who pay property and school taxes to pay twice, the building and maintenance upkeep. The job of an elected official, no matter the government level, is to explain to the people what public capital represents and the reasons why it is needed, not to obtain underhanded funds; I am basically saying, "the people who elect servants to office, to serve the people and the surrounding areas, should know what elected officials are doing with their money, i.e., public funds." If elected governor of Texas, I will insist, state agencies and proxies, their mission change to one worthy of being a state agency or trusted proxy, and open the process up to include both county governments and individual taxpayers who have real ideas applicable to surrounding counties but could also be ideas used throughout the state. There are more than a few, many, state agencies and proxies that cannot justify their existence; they will have to give up 30 percent of budget funds for the newly created county skills funds. I am adamant about focusing 30 percent of time, energy, and resources into the new priorities of Texas to get 120 percent production from individual taxpayers, advantaged citizens, disadvantaged citizens, and education endeavors—modified Pareto principle.

No matter the amount in the economic stabilization fund, 30 percent is what will be placed on the statewide referendum because individual taxpayers deserve it. I am tired of all the feckless maneuverings that amounts to no real dollars for hardworking Texans. The governor, lieutenant governor, and state legislature, i.e., tax collectors, will team up in their coterie and paint this nightmarish scenario about my plan for Texas. If you have not noticed, we are already in a perpetual nightmare—unaffordable pathways to success, unaffordable health insurance, and 0 percent returns on personal savings. This is what the "clique" should be focused on, right? I will admit chaos on their part because they're wrangling over nothing, which is the problem; all that needs to be done is release the money to each county skills fund, if I am blessed to be governor of Texas, how hard is that? I do not know if anyone remembers the unprecedented creative destruction that happened in the recording industry in the late 1990s and early 2000s, but everyone was trying to figure out how to accommodate and compensate all the players in the industry, all because of the idea of purchasing songs instead of albums over the internet, now the movie industry will be experiencing the same dynamic due to streaming services. What I am getting at are the struggles behind the scene, but I will keep all Texans informed on the implementation of the big deal legislation for our new life if honored to be the servant leader of Texas. There will be clear differences from business precedent because it will be the "state government" fighting to hold on to old governing traditions, customs, myths, lore, and money for useless projects, but the tumult will be worth it. Just remember, this will be the same governor, lieutenant governor, and state legislature, i.e., tax collectors, who talk about tax cuts and freedom. Pressure each one of these elected officials about this "hypocrisy" as to why "Texans cannot benefit financially from helping others in their community", with strong state backing?

As a voter in all elections, especially state and county, I look for politicians to do what is necessary and effective to put "real cash" back into our pockets, not rebates, tax cuts, or exemptions; this is the test I use, but everyone seems to fail. The person with the imagination, vision, and plan for the future has no agenda for the elites, corporations, unions, etc., only for individual taxpayers and community, so the person I would have easily voted for remains constrained, though, no fault of his or her own. If the voters of Texas (Republic) will give me the chance to lead "a new south" into a new era of "enlightened reconstruction" that invites all regardless of political beliefs to join in community investment where we live for the improvement of life, your bottom line and decreased property and school taxes will prevail. It is "what you see is what you get." I see before others see, I see far beyond others, and I see bigger than others. No one talks like me about our life and love. Francis Bacon once stated, "If we are to achieve things never before accomplished, we must employ methods never before attempted." And this historic campaign is all about an effort to imagine things that seem impossible to be possible, because it is!

Thirty percent of the rainy day fund and select state bureaucracies will give equity to the institution of community necessary for twenty-first century transformational autonomy-locally, to begin. When these actions are taken, our great state will set precedent for the "other 49", and the world, by giving individual taxpayers the upper hand in building a brighter future for themselves and communities across Texas.

Businesses have a well-established persistent pattern of having concern for themselves—profit and layoffs when necessary, tax abatements, defined contribution plans, and the support of the state and county governments. And to some extent, I have no problem with it. Texans, my problem lies with the fact that there is no well-established persistent pattern for the institution of community to offset businesses and any unforeseen insignificant practices. The way through all the problems and favoritism in state governance is to allow profitability at all levels within Texas bureaucracy, wherever state aid is involved. The front-end will be for individual taxpayers to invest in academic development, skilled vocational trades, and necessary support tools for success in county citizenry; the back-end will be for businesses to use to their advantage because they will no longer have to concern themselves with training skilled workers.

To protect the institution of community is "binding in my conscience" because it is owed to ordinary Texans who pay property and school taxes every year without any fanfare or reward for doing what is expected. Individual taxpayers must be given a "home-grown" strategy that promotes improvement and development in their communities forevermore. We can ensure a lifelong commitment to what is necessary for Texans, so, to have the right amount of experience and to carry on responsibly—health insurance, life insurance, savings, property and school taxes, and continuing education (i.e., more skilled vocational trades or higher education). Transforming citizenry to such heights requires an immovable determination that cannot be bargained with or cajoled. It is time to share 30 percent of the economic stabilization fund and select state agencies' budgets with the communities across Texas. I am made of effort, toil, and thinking, which lends itself to thoughts of hope and understanding for our fellow Texans. We can eliminate the distance between us, create harmony, and drastically reduce all social ills by giving our communities what they need most—purpose.

Every legislative year, I want to ensure every county approximately $11 to $15 million alongside the counties' contribution to their skills fund to begin our journey to be known as the world's problem solvers because of the real commitment to community investment. The greatest piece of legislation ever written was the GI Bill; it gave people a chance to improve their lives in all manner of areas from skilled vocational trades to advanced degrees. The flaw that has always been apparent, in my opinion, in all the great social legislation is a lack of individual taxpayer incentive—a pathway for all to win. You see, because of the freedom of movement, in my plan, someone must be able to invest in each citizens' formable years to obtain a solid academic foundation and adult life to ensure, at minimum, one skilled vocational trade, producing a taxpaying citizen who is capable of taking care of themselves and a family wherever they decide to live. So if a citizen decides to leave the county for whatever reason, unfortunately, the potential tax dollars are eliminated, therefore, creating reciprocity through investment, offset any movement of adults and families.

Envision the economic stabilization fund doing exactly what it is supposed to do—encourage Texans to go all-out by investing in their communities, which in turn invokes the passionate feelings of one family, one people, and one Texas. We will never know the power of our economic might until all GOD's children, created in his image, are included. And when this happens, our blessings will transform misfortune into exceeding abundance that sustains itself in all communities across Texas. If Texans want responsible people—invest. If Texans want taxpaying citizens—invest. If Texans want to eradicate poverty—invest. If Texans want affordable health care—invest. Whatever Texans feel the need for in their community—invest.

Everyone must know the importance of the economic stabilization fund because it represents a better life for all, if used right. We need Texans focused and motivated in their communities making money and solving age-old problems the state has no intention of solving; GOD is community and wants nothing less, for His magnificent creation, than for His people to not only dwell in it but thrive in it.

Remember this, Jack Daniel Foster Jr. is a thinker and recognizes state bureaucracy cannot do what is naturally intended for community, so, investment strategies will use efforts such as "enthusiasms" that will give individual taxpayers and buy-in citizens a platform to improve their community and bottom line through investment in social good—education and empowerment. It will never be economically or socially right, just, or fair without the participation of ordinary Texans in building their prosperity and the things that matter most in our society—education, health care, and retirement. If you want Texans to care, make them part of the solution. Understand, state bureaucracy will have to prove its worth with 70%, while I make my point with 30%, i.e., effectively and efficiently, with the work of individual taxpayer investors.

CHAPTER 6

The Economic-Financial Model—the Big Picture

Leaders touch a heart before they ask for a hand.
—*21 Irrefutable Laws of Leadership* (tenth law)

THE MESSAGE

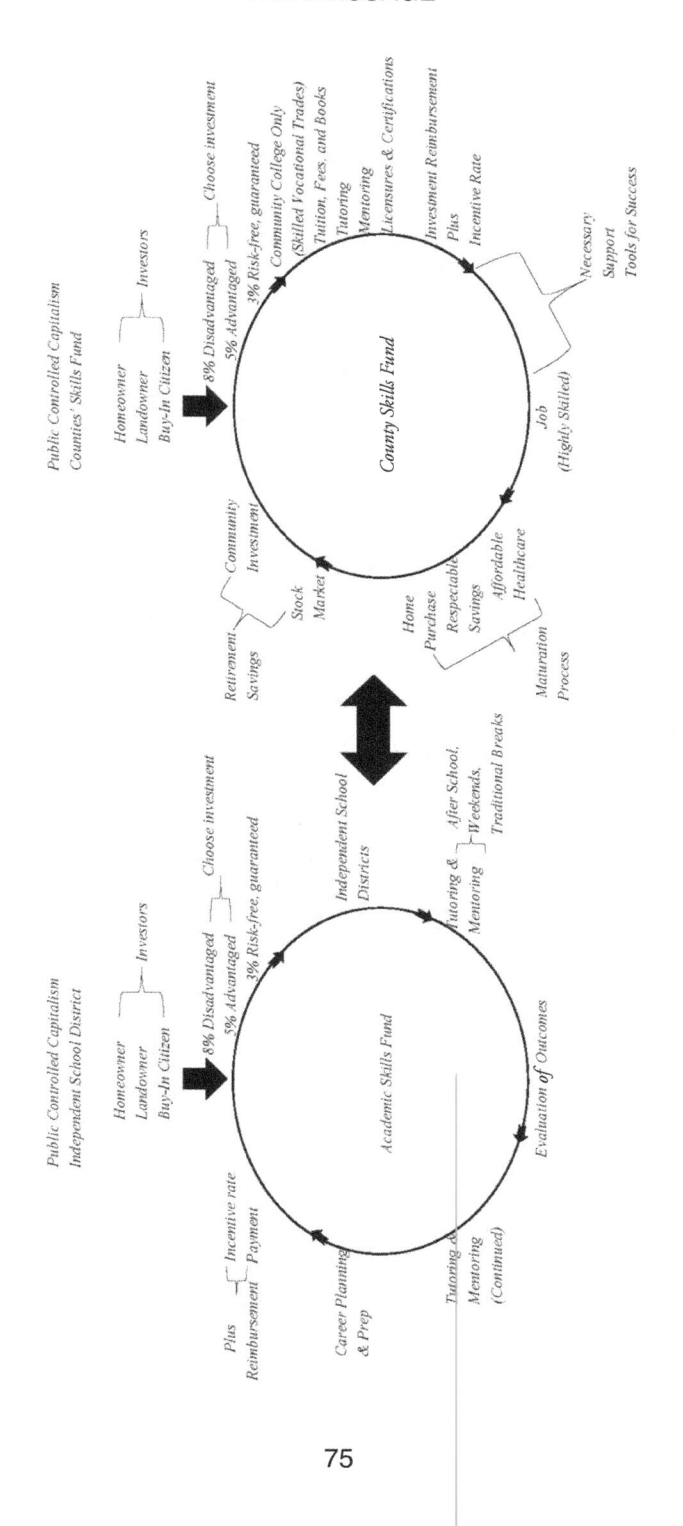

As I discuss the combined effects of both the academic skills fund and county skills fund in every Texas county, like my beloved county on p.74, imagine what this will do for all socioeconomic groups in our state—wealthy, middle-class, marginalized, children, and immigrants, classified together in my lexicon—"the quintet". The first noble thing we can do for communities across Texas is to establish foundational roots in education through real investment, which will ensure the necessary confidence, knowledge, vocational training, and belief in oneself. The second, and probably the loftiest act of all time, is springboarding from the first noble deed of investment to giving a seamlessly conscious, tangible "set of assurances", p.75, that will aid in unleashing the creative destruction that I know is within every Texan. This is the precipice of greatness, unbounded sureties, and unheralded economic-financial might that will be brought forth by homeowners, landowners, and buy-in citizens who will do what is only meant for them to do—spread, highly valued, wisdom and support every aspect of knowledge building & sharing in their communities. The design is clear, citizens who pay property and school taxes, or the median of both, in the new future of Texas are meant to be the leaders and, in doing so, set the bar for all Texans to strive for.

When both investment tools (i.e., academic skills fund and county skills fund) are readily available for homeowners, landowners, and buy-in citizenry to improve lives through bona fide investment in their communities, we will have arrived at a place very close to King Solomon's kingdom where there was no lack, and the peoples' needs met. I say this with great clarity looking forward without hesitation, taming the "big three" (i.e., education, health-care premiums, and respectable return rates on savings are paramount to an indivisible Texas).

I am offering something unique in the annals of Texas politics without placing one socioeconomic group above another, giving every Texan purpose in their community. In the quintet (i.e., wealthy, middle-class, marginalized, children, and immigrants), each group has a task to ameliorate and enrich the life of the other. The fields are ripe with an economic and financial harvest from my perspective. We decrease unemployment through the legitimacy of skilled vocational trades and technical skills. We increase wages naturally because of value and drastically reduce opportunity costs. There is no alternative better than investing resources into Texans; an environment is created for ordinary county citizens to have investment opportunities countywide in local people to increase their knowledge, wisdom, and also relieve the pressure of kitchen table issues with more cash.

Wealthy Texans can be assured a respectable return at home in any community within their county by investing in county citizenry for skilled vocational trades that are relevant and essential to the times or help build solid academic foundations in local public schools. Your county and state need you not only to invest in companies and Wall Street; we need you to impact real lives—guide, lead, and show our citizens how to become responsible taxpaying citizens. I do not want the wealthy to be rich in vain, show us the power of what money can do.

Middle-class citizens, literally, stand to gain the most in my plan for the enhancement of their lives (i.e., pocketbook issues—education, health care, and increase returns on savings) through investment opportunities in oneself, family, and community. Most taxes, by far, are paid by the middle-class, so it behooves state government to direct all enthusiasm toward this central category. The whole point of the academic skills fund and the county skills fund is to create a space where middle-class citizens can constructively impart knowledge and wisdom, thus, benefiting financially to protect themselves and their posterity; the middle-class is the cornerstone for all efforts.

Marginalized citizens this is your time; all perceptible efforts will be focused, toward elevating you, through an incentive rate of 8 percent, so, this means citizens who pay property and school taxes or the median of both will do whatever is necessary for your success to obtain certifications and licenses in skilled vocational training programs, which could be local or anywhere in the state, depending on the specialized vocational training curriculums. Do not worry about financial aid or student loans; your investor will handle everything and be compensated. Just study hard and absorb all the knowledge in the skilled vocational trade program selected, and wisdom offered by your investor. It is imperative that you become an essential part of your county, paying property and school taxes, also handling the necessary responsibilities that your county and state will depend on in reconstructing a new future for communities, Texans, and Texas.

The children of Texas will only know "shared interest" from their community, something mothers' and expectant mothers' long for privately in their hearts. They want to know everything in the states' power will be done to ensure their child's well-being through education, life development, and careers. Look at the economic-financial model carefully, this will be our incorruptible inheritance and legacy to all that come after fellow citizens in their community and county. Any deficiency, academically or lack, will be handled through investment after school, on weekends, and during traditional summer break. The point is either the parents take care of it and get the incentive rate or someone else can, with permission. Nobody falls out of consideration, too much is at stake now. In the economic-financial model, the left side, the academic skills fund is structured to allow individual taxpayers to get our youth the necessary help needed, one-on-one, to build a strong academic foundation, and the process should be repeated over and over when problems arise. Once the children of Texas get to secondary education, the same form of investment continues in academic deficiencies, but as they progress from middle to late secondary, it is time to introduce careers in skilled vocational trades and how to methodically leverage skilled trade careers into traditional college to pay for it themselves instead of student loans. The, 21st century, standard moving forward as a child of Texas will be the understanding of responsible choices through knowledge, wisdom, and maturation—letting community canons invest first in your life, reciprocities, in primary-secondary, and post-secondary education at the community college level for relevant skilled trades or technical skills. And the imparting of "real-world" knowledge and wisdom that can be used for a lifetime. The same investment standards hold once primary, and secondary education is completed except incentive rates will now flow from the right side—the county skills fund. The children of Texas will be accustomed to improving their lives through skilled vocational training programs by either paying for it themselves and receiving reimbursement plus incentive rate or using the customary individual taxpayer investor channel first, by allowing the stalwarts of community to receive reimbursement plus, financial and social amenities. No one will be surprised at how the new Texas wields its economic might and influence for Texans. All the children of Texas will have to do is obtain a solid academic foundation, remain dedicated and motivated in continuing their education, let community shepherds invest, and pay close attention to wisdom, so incorruptible inheritance and legacy can endure.

Immigrants, new Texans in any county or destination in Texas, we will consider your child or children part of Texas now, so investment in your child, or children, who have academic deficiencies or lack of any kind, will be a natural occurrence by individual taxpayer investors, and the same goes for adult arrivals; individual taxpayers will ensure the necessary investment in your education for skilled vocational trades, technical skills, and associate degrees through the county skills fund. Do not let any of this frighten you in your new land. Communities in Texas must establish equity in your life and child, or children to have the freedoms and earning power everyone in Texas strives for.

Ask yourself this question: Where does public money serve the best good? In my opinion, accounting tricks such as tax rebates, tax exemptions, tax abatements, etc. create a "winners and losers" environment with "our money" that strangely begins to erode the social garland in our communities and increase burdens on an already fraught middle class, impoverished community, children, and immigrant population. We defeat the tradition of giveaway governing in every form and fashion by using the Economic-financial model that will be firmly embedded in every county and school district to propel homeowners, landowners, and buy-in citizens to do the exact opposite of traditional giveaway governing. Without the accounting tricks, winners and losers are eliminated from the public sector's money, to be used wisely in local communities so ordinary citizens who pay property and school taxes or the median of both can now receive principal reimbursements and constructive cash (i.e., incentive rates to support the power to help others). Public money has not been used right since the concept was conceived; we are supposed to develop solutions to problems that encourage community action; it should be understood that Texans are essential to the states' business; the quintet is the affirmative link to social good, if used right.

The arrow between the academic skills fund and county skills fund signals the ease in which homeowners, landowners, and buy-in citizens can use these investment tools in their domiciled county and the flexibility of the model allows for inclusion of prisoners for investment throughout the state, to enrich their lives as well. The quintessential piece that will make public-controlled capitalism work in both the academic skills fund and the county skills fund is the risk-free rate. I expect every homeowner, landowner, and buy-in citizen who choose to participate to give their all to fellow citizens and to know that "principal compensation" will be built-in, plus the risk-free rate should something go wrong because it is "the impossible" coupled with a "Financial smoothing gradation" that is sorely needed to give citizens a sense, or inkling, there is a future leader striving to swing the pendulum back toward common folks.

As I talk about the big picture, continue thinking about how these two combined investment tools in every county will promote the institution of community and will ease burdens and concerns for family, friends, poor, children, immigrants, and prisoners. The old adage "There is no shame in being poor, the shame is in not doing anything about it", will be dealt a serious blow. I believe the Economic-financial model, the big picture, will deliver a conclusive end to the old saying. Our hearts tell us that it is time for something transformational that will unite Texans, like my plan, which will create and encourage educational environments for all Texans to step forward at any time, whether for investment purposes or to absorb knowledge and wisdom. Moments that transcend division are the recipes for generating indescribable economic, financial, and intellectual might that extend beyond the edge of our universe into the unknown (i.e., super universe), the statement cannot be disproven, because it has never been attempted. This is the puissance that will build great communities, in my opinion, individual taxpayers are being restrained, contained, hindered, blocked, bottled-up, etc. by tradition and customs, so we lose valuable time, day after day, month after month, and year after year, in solving the mysteries to our most challenging issues.

Private corporations do not truly believe in state government, so they look for any way possible to not pay their fair share at the county level, and our state government is more than happy to capitulate; businesses can be made to believe in making communities strong again through both investment tools, as individual taxpayers, they will be able to invest in county citizenry "first-hand", so they will know as workers and administrators the worth of what is taking place in communities across Texas. In three to five years after both academic skills and county skills fund have reached maturity, corporations will begin inquiring about relocation to Texas. The educational level, investment level, tax level, and employment level, i.e., all levels referring to every county, will pay unimaginable dividends in personal prosperity, profits for businesses, and increase tax revenues for county and state to reinvest in communities, again and again.

Our communities without transformative financial tools to create purpose and unity will continue to cultivate ruin and leave all capacities limited, but if we begin now, "retooling" the institutions that are intended to lay the foundation for strong communities, independent school districts and county governments, we can get back into the secret door—peoples' hearts—to reclaim new horizons and social trust. Do not underestimate the power of hope within security, i.e., repair and reward, a state of being that will unbridle the human spirit in such a way to surrender the mind to "advantaged thought," an elevated thinking process that can be fostered in any socioeconomic group, but it has to be tempered with knowledge and wisdom driven by homeowners, landowners, and buy-in citizens. It is always easier for the tax collectors to use top-down policy, top-down economics, and top-down state contracts, no thinking involved. Advantaged thought makes citizens of Texas valuable to our state, county, and most importantly, communities; there has to be "special environments" that can be collectively accepted by all Texans where everyone can do their part and benefit from it, 30%—Rainy Day Fund. I believe in a strong state government but not to dominate the citizens that make our state great, it has more to do with developing solutions that favor a preferred destination for all Texans.

We must channel our outrage, caused by traditional governing, into productivity for "self and others" in the Economic-Financial model to show how much time and resources state bureaucracy has harmed real incomes, affordable health care, and return rates on savings, i.e., the infrastructure of life, this has nothing to do with private industries or the federal government. Our elected state officials like to "marry" state and federal issues together when it suits their cause, think about the "major questions doctrine". My message is for Texans to know that an ordinary citizen, Jack Daniel Foster, Jr., cares about the plight of all Texans, regardless of their socioeconomic status. A person of means can be used more effectively and efficiently than a state agency, which is mandated to use "means testing" to determine whether a citizen is worthy of help or not to become a taxpaying citizen. Does it make any sense? Because it makes perfect sense to the tax collectors. Individual taxpayers will quickly adapt to researching careers for investees, securing the best-skilled vocational trade programs, staying in constant contact with investees, ensuring overall success through certifications or licensure at our trusted community colleges, and getting paid their principal plus incentive rate or risk-free rate, therefore, fulfilling the heart and pocketbook of individual taxpayers and giving investees (i.e., county citizenry) real income capacity with an unlimited future, a "set of assurances", p.75, for all Texans. The same scenario will emerge for individual taxpayers over and over again in both academic skills fund and county skills fund; in fact, becoming more efficient each time in elevating citizens to new heights albeit children or adults. Think long, hard and be imaginative about what a "new Texas" for Texans would look like with ordinary citizens taking a role in one another's life will be in three to five years. If our elected officials really cared about Texans, they would be more creative, imaginative, innovative, and insightful, all to unleash your power to protect our republic. What has to be remembered is their thought process—protect the republic, not Texans. The only way to protect the republic is to have a strong people who have the ability to improve their lives through common folks in their community despite socioeconomic status, zip code, circumstances, race, barriers erected, etc. State agencies will never have the love and concern for your community as you do, this is why it is urgently important to give individual taxpayer investors the financial tools for "transformative action".

Our lives must be placed back into the hands of our communities and there is no better way to ensure Texans get what is needed for success than at home, but the governor, lieutenant governor, state legislators, state agencies, and state proxies, i.e., tax collectors, insist on perverse financial incentives, for individual taxpayers. What else do we call leading the nation in uninsured people, trapping our citizens in low-wage jobs, increased poverty in one-third of Texas counties, student loans in community colleges, inequity, and selfishness, i.e., an assumption against interest, not for? It is a direct insult to the citizens of Texas to endure more of the same illogical status quo, that do not even benefit the wealthy or middle class. There are no concrete answers as to why we remain on the same trajectory as fifty years ago—tradition, customs, or lore? I want a Texas that works for everyone, progresses with the times naturally, and has a long reach through the tireless commitment of homeowners, landowners, and buy-in citizens who will have the incentives to pursue it, do not concern yourself with state bureaucracy—30% budget cut, because the economic-financial model will be full of economic and financial benefits that will be tangible—cash for the investors, real income for county citizenry, declining unemployment, communities working together efficiently and effectively, dramatic decrease in crime, and fully funded community colleges. The unseen economic and financial benefits are a recession-proof dynamic, driven purpose, social trust, increase tax revenue for both county and state, peace of mind-financial security, risk-free three percent, and incorruptible inheritance for all Texans.

Think about the impact and statement we make by putting everything else aside and focusing on what matters most—communities and Texans. When we make the Economic-Financial model a standard-bearer for every independent school district and county in Texas, all attention will be back on our state for the right reasons.

Perceptions of our vast state will quickly give way to a keen interest in how homeowners, landowners, and buy-in citizens are able to
repair communities through education and life experiences, and be
rewarded for performing these sacred tasks, until the end of time, it
will always remain necessary for Texans to "look forward to the next
day." We need the quintet (i.e., wealthy, middle-class, marginalized,
children, and immigrants) to "do the things you think you cannot,"
as former First Lady Eleanor Roosevelt states. Think on a grand scale
for the sake of Texans, community, county, big and small businesses,
environment (air, land, and water), oil and gas, Texas, and our lives.

Dr. Martin Luther King once stated, "Human progress never
rolls in easy on the backs of inevitability." I agree with his obser-
vation of the struggle in the twentieth century and, unfortunately,
the present day-twenty-first century. Our problem with unavoidable
progression has always been the use of government to elevate the
conditions of one group or two at the expense of others, so actions
begin to be misconstrued, unfortunately as favoritisms. The moral of
the story is applicable to the toil in the world—the rich having it all,
the poor losing hope, and the middle-class caught in the proverbial
middle. It is the Economic-Financial model that provides a direct
proportional response to the question of advancement and relief by
encouraging 21st century transformational autonomy at the local
level—the central place where our lives begin. No Texan should ever
be made to feel that they must turn their backs on community in-or-
der to be successful in life. The Economic-Financial model reassures,
citizens, that you never lose your love and concern for community
and county, no matter where you decide to live in Texas, by providing a guarantee of principal and a risk-free rate. This is the state to
show the "other forty-nine" and the entire world how to superimpose
a financial super-structure, within all counties, to benefit individual taxpayer investors and recipients, so to bridge all socioeconomic
barriers to produce a mutual exchange of privileges that will bring
Texans much-deserved security in the present and future. I am basically saying, "Courage is the power to let go of the familiar" and
allow the Economic-Financial model to incentivize individual citizens to "vest" in their community "to skill people up," whether they

happen to be school-age or adults. It is about the quality of time and effort in peoples' lives that will make the difference, empowerment, that I seek.

I am comfortable with any peril we are facing from environmental to penury and everything in between; the confidence comes from having a plan that gives power to individual citizens in the present to prepare citizenry for tomorrow. Our state government is fragmented purposely with an intent to keep power dispersed among the governor, lieutenant governor, state agencies, and legislative committees, so no matter how hard they try, the dysfunction is too great. This is why it will remain steadfast to have a new governor that recognizes how to operate in an immovable, recalcitrant environment. I will place insurmountable pressure on the "Tax collectors" with my message in the form of a book, a statewide referendum, my legislative agenda, and my unyielding conviction that will "alchemize" the conversation; all this for individual taxpaying citizens to take their rightful place and do good works in their community. Paul Coelho stated, "There are some things in life worth fighting for to the end." For Jack Daniel Foster, Jr., it will always be for homeowners, landowners, and buy-in citizens to take care of their communities, without yielding.

Here is an illuminating sense of my thought process compared to someone else. We have so many jobs in cybersecurity that cannot be filled, and companies have resorted to hiring outside the United States. If I was servant leader of Texas, I would instruct our community colleges to send representatives to the US State Department, US Department of Defense, and National Intelligence Agency to figure out what type of academic curriculum would be acceptable for national certification at the community college level, and of course, universities can do the same for upper-level studies, but this is about individual taxpaying citizens using the investment tools within the Economic-Financial model to assist local citizenry in their community to obtain good-paying jobs that would require skilled vocational training in Texas community colleges for national credentialing. The individual taxpaying citizen will provide all the necessary supports toward the certification (books, tuition, tutors) and receive principal investment plus, an incentive rate of 8 percent if the investee is disadvantaged, and 5 percent if the investee is advantaged; if something should go wrong with the investee, there will always be a guarantee of 3 percent. Everything has to involve individual taxpayers who pay property and school taxes or the median of both because no one really knows where FAFSA, Sallie Mae, and private student loan money really comes from; no face, so no real accountability. The Economic-Financial model will ensure investors and investees talk to one another and see the human side of things, such as the importance of health insurance, retirement savings, and continuing education—all lifelong odysseys.

Make sure to stay focused on your pocketbook as tax collectors talk about the same traditional governance and economics that has nothing to do with ordinary Texans because there has yet to be any easing of kitchen table issues. The Economic-Financial model brings human infrastructure matters to the forefront (i.e., real income, affordable health care, respectable return on savings) and renders divisive issues pliable or tolerable as we move forward in our lives. Follow my intuition closely, without the pressures of a reliable alternative to work with traditional institutions in-favor of community uncertainty will continue to loom. In order for the Economic-Financial model to work for individual homeowners, landowners, and buy-in citizens, we must make every effort to invest mightily in our communities for something money could never extinguish, the instinctive propensity to improve oneself or station in life. The extrinsic values (i.e., principal plus incentive rate or principal plus risk-free rate) are the easy parts. What cannot be quantitated, only perceived, is the intrinsic worth unleashed by an intuitive plan that can capture broken hearts, flourishing minds, and the indelible human spirit in our communities, counties, and Texas. Property and school taxes will continue to cycle in and out of our counties, money never seen, with some county dollars being dispersed back to the state capitol for more giveaways; no breaks for the "true" taxpayer, only routine tax increases, not decreases, that are ultimately "ordered-downward" by the state comptroller through the county appraisal district. Remember, "they are not done with common people yet", because in addition to county taxes, we still have licensing fees, tolls, Medicaid taxes, and a host of consumption taxes with no relief for personal finances. They have enough nerve to talk about the state budget as if it is "State earned income". Yes, the oil companies pay state permit fees, and yes, their fees also support, 85%, the economic stabilization fund, but that means nothing to most people. The pool of public money, "our money," is dispensed to state bureaucracy and proxies for contracts. I do not have a problem with their process per se; my problem is with leaving the most important people, within our traditions and customs governing process, out of the "compensation loop" to improve their lives and prepare others for the future.

Some things will always be out of our control in life, but we can fix certain life-altering mechanisms, processes, or systems, by isolating the community economy, p.25, and delivering on a "set of assurances", p.75, that will work to the benefit of all communities and Texans; remember, we are not "changing capitalism", just transforming it by entering the farthest or most remote part of its borders, i.e., "exigent"—capitalism, so 21st Century Transformation Autonomy can take-hold in our communities. Keep in mind, the economic-financial model will perpetually make our state better, bigger, inclusive, stronger, and use a "security element" placed on living a quality life and imparting knowledge and wisdom to others. The question has to be asked of oneself: What is the true purpose of our existence, really? I am certain it has nothing to do with money, political battles, or oppression techniques. In my humble opinion, our GOD-given purpose is to create socioeconomic environments that are conducive to mending hearts, facing and defeating challenges, sharing, caring, and being the best Christian, Texan, and American we can be.

In the Bible, 2 Corinthians 1:3–4 states that "GOD blesses his people, so they may bless those who have yet to be blessed." In other words, if you are one of the fortunate Texans-blessed, I will use all my conviction, might, and passion, coupled with the power of the state if elected servant leader of Texas (i.e., governor of Texas), to see-to-it "The ground is fertile for what lies ahead." The higher Texans want to climb the more Texans need leadership; I will strengthen homeowners, landowners, and buy-in citizens' hand in preparation for the climb.

STATEWIDE REFERENDUM: GOVERNOR'S NEW AUTHORITY

1. The 30 percent rule—30 percent of the economic stabilization fund (i.e., rainy day fund; use money to fund county skills funds, 254 counties, every legislative year).
2. The 30 percent rule—30 percent of state agencies' and proxies' budgets-that do not impact the lives of ordinary citizens; use money to fund county skills funds, 254 counties, every legislative year.
3. Appointment of state's attorney general of Texas.
4. Appointment of state's comptroller of Texas.

This will allow the new governor of Texas to effectively maneuver in any given situation, thus, impacting all Texans' lives the right way.

BIG DEAL LEGISLATION

All items fall under the economic-finance model.

1. Create a skills fund in every county for homeowners, landowners, and buy-in citizens to invest in communities within their domiciled county for education purposes to improve lives.
2. Independent school districts will create an academic skills fund for homeowners, landowners, and buy-in citizens to invest in primary and secondary education to build strong academic foundations and career readiness for every youth within their domiciled county.
3. Skills fund and academic skills fund will be maintained separately from all county and independent school district(s) budgets; funds will only be used for principal, i.e., expenditures, and incentive rate pay.
4. County treasurer and county clerk are to maintain an accurate account balance for the county skills fund, working closely with CPC and may assist the independent school district.
5. Every skills fund and academic skills fund will use the concept of public-controlled capitalism; 8 percent return for disadvantaged citizens, 5 percent return for advantaged citizens, and a risk-free rate of 3 percent to guarantee investment in every community (floor).
6. Create a Community Protection Commission to supervise, validate records, and issue payments to homeowners, landowners, and buy-in citizens. Five citizens will be on the commission to be rotated every three years and begin train-

ing replacement in year two. Racial makeup will resemble the demographic of county; these will be salaried positions, and the Community Protection Commission will be appointed by the commissioners' court. Community Protection Commission may assist and share records with the independent school district in the county.

7. County contributions are as follows: rural county, $2 million every legislative year; urban counties, $5 million per million of the population every legislative year; and both rural and urban counties will determine depletion rate of both academic/county skills funds and re-evaluate contribution level.

8. Investors are to be paid their initial investment money plus the incentive rate at the end of the investment period (i.e., depending on the length of the education program invested), but the time frame can be no less than a year and a day or maximum of three years.

9. Automatic eligibility for homeowners and landowners to invest in domiciled county citizenry.

10. Buy-in citizens must pay the median property and school tax every year to maintain eligibility to invest in domiciled county citizenry.

11. Can only invest in three citizens at a time, but deals can be made with other homeowners and landowners to increase to a maximum of six citizens to invest for skilled vocational trades if there are possible delinquencies in property and school taxes.

12. All taxes must be paid in full for the year, October–January 31.

13. Must live in the domiciled county of the investee.

14. Every homeowner, landowner, and buy-citizen may invest in a maximum of two prisoners every year for skilled vocational trades across the state—no boundaries preclude investment, and incentive rates are the same as county skills fund and academic skills fund.

15. Community Colleges will set up skilled vocational trade programs of relevance with the Texas Department of Corrections-Huntsville's input. No student loans, only investment dollars from homeowners, landowners, and buy-in citizens. All prisoners must have a GED before advancement into skilled programs, all investors must work with the state comptroller, county tax offices, and CPC.

16. No investments in county citizenry are eligible for payment outside the affiliation of community colleges.

17. Broadband cable construction throughout the whole state supervised by a newly created commission—the quintet.

18. Increase income threshold for Medicaid—$60,000—begin to gradually decrease in three to five years after the county skills fund has been given time to show results.

19. Eliminate 75 percent of County abatements throughout the state.

20. Double electrical grid capacity and weatherize all essential utilities and appoint the quintet to the PUC, rotate every three years.

21. Redirect 30 percent lottery tax revenue from foundation school fund to independent school districts in the establishment of academic skills fund—divide equally among 1,025 ISD's–plus.

22. Redirect 100 percent sin tax to aid in independent school districts' establishment of academic skills fund—divide equally among 1,025 ISD's–plus.

23. Modify insurance commissioner's health insurance regulatory authority.

24. To properly be a community investor, i.e., homeowner, landowner or buy-in citizen, the Texan must be 35 years or older.

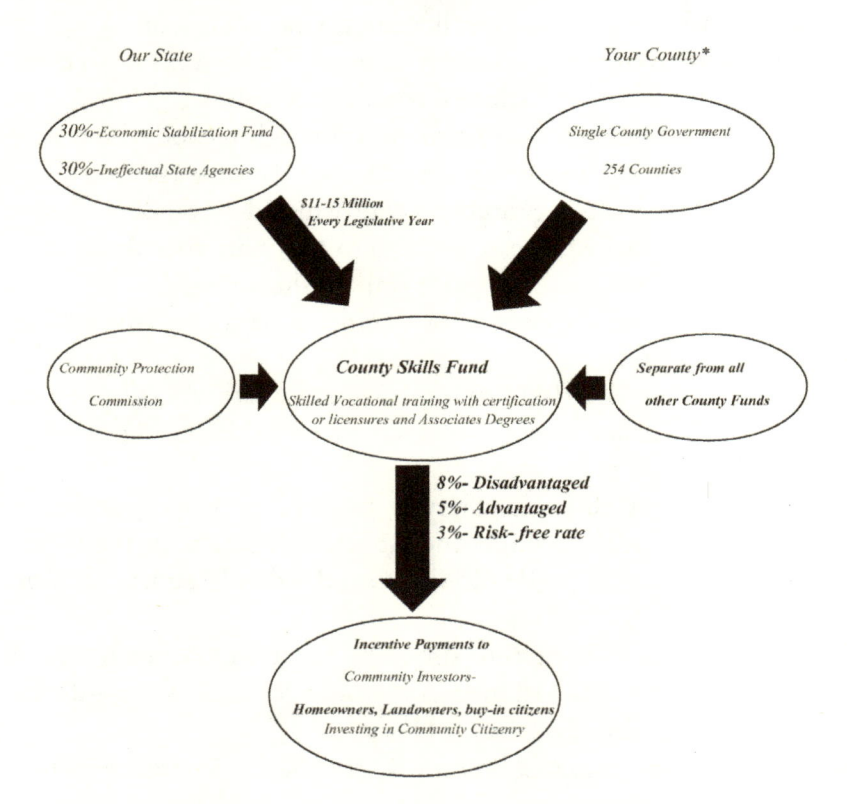

Funding Flow for Public Controlled Capitalism

County Skills Fund

Urban Counties- Add $5 million for One Million population every legislative year, depletion rate to be determined over a few years.

Rural Counties- Add $2 Million every legislative year, depletion rate to be determined over a few years.

The AIM is to keep the Skills Fund Safe and Solvent for Homeowners, Landowners, and Buy-in Citizens to continue investing in Community Citizenry throughout domiciled county.

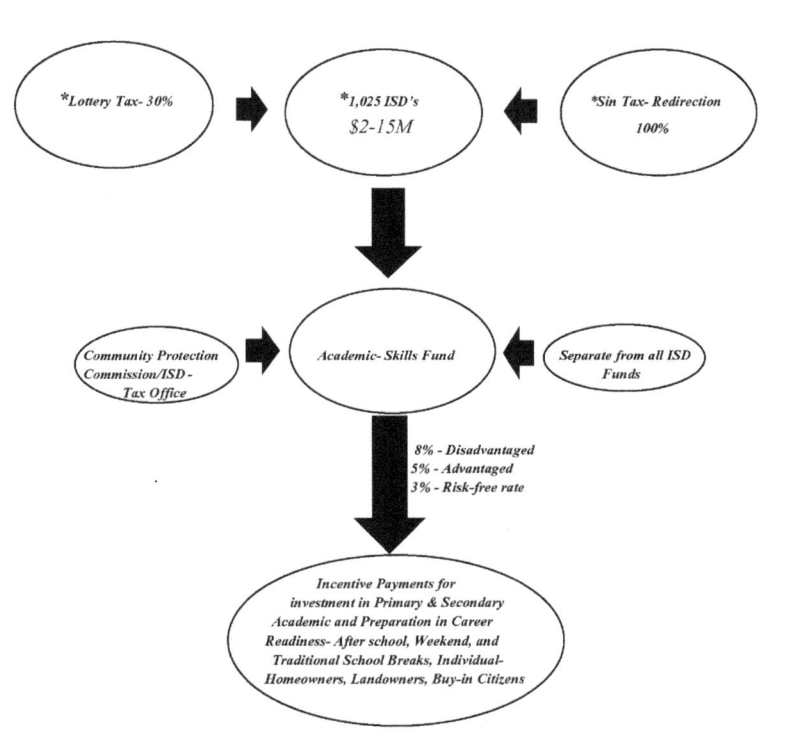

Funding Flow for Public Controlled Capitalism

Independent School Districts

30%-Lottery tax revenue will be redirected from the Foundation School Fund to be divided equally among the 1,025 ISD's- aid in establishment of Academic-Skills Fund.
Independent School Districts will establish an Academic-Skills Fund for Homeowners, Landowners and Buy-citizens to begin investing in student's academic and career preparedness. Rural- $2 Million; Urban- $15 Million, depletion rate to be determined.
100%-Sin Tax revenue will be redirected to 1,025 ISD's- aid in the establishment of Academic-Skills Fund.

All school districts along with lottery and sin tax revenues will be committed to funding a safe and solvent Academic-Skills Fund for Homeowners, Landowners, and Buy-in citizens to keep investing in our future taxpayers- every legislative year.

SOURCES

Maxwell, John. *21 Irrefutable Laws of Leadership*. New York: HarperCollins Leadership, 2007.

Bureau of Census Research. "Highest Poverty Rates in U.S." 2018.

US Constitution: Preamble

Quotes

Alan Turning
Charles De Gaulle
Albert Einstein
George Washington Carver
Paul Coelho
Dr. Martin Luther King
Former First Lady Eleanor Roosevelt
Edmund Burke
Adam Smith
Francis Bacon

Bible Verses

Proverbs 31:10–11
First Corinthians 1:27
Romans 8:28
Jeremiah 22:1–5
John 15:16
Mathew 7:24–27
Second Corinthians 1:3–4
Luke 18:1

ABOUT THE AUTHOR

I am a servant of *God*, watchman by nature, and romantic; I am a state-certified teacher in biology and economics, hold a master's degree in finance, and became a certified retirement counselor, but education tells you nothing about my heart, discernment capacity, and intuition. I yearn for a school of thought that utilizes all in a "capitalistic way" to ensure we will always be a society that replenishes itself the right way in every community across Texas. It is necessary to set a new standard in twenty-first century leadership. So I have decided not only to run for the Forward Party-Texas gubernatorial nomination in 2026, but also to release my message in book form and, simultaneously, to make my imagination, vision, and plan inescapable.

I believe, when reading *The Message: A Time for Repair and Reward in Texas Communities*, a person must imagine the plenipotentiary handed down by the "new" Texas to embolden all aspects of life. The power shared will aspire individuals to suspend all negative forces to build toward the unknown together.

Printed in the USA
CPSIA information can be obtained
at www.ICGtesting.com
LVHW090246230324
775311LV00001B/175

9 781638 606581